The Forgiving Lifestyle

How to Forgive Everyone (Including Yourself)

The Forgiving Lifestyle

How to Forgive Everyone (Including Yourself)

Marina Michaels

Athena Star Press
Santa Rosa, California

Contents

Preface

We are all looking for peace, one way or another. But although there are as many ways to find peace as there are people on this planet (and maybe more), many haven't found it. So many of us are still in conflict with others, fighting battles large and small, taking offense at what people say or do, or at what we think they said or did. We are confused, angry, hurt—many times because someone did something to us, but sometimes because someone simply did something we didn't like, something that had nothing to do with us.

Without getting too philosophical, I think that this is all because many messages of peace and of how to live a peaceful life just put people off because of how they are written or because they say something people just can't agree with. If you are turned off by a message, it isn't going to be much good, is it?

I have been told many times in my life that I am the most objective and rational person someone has met. Perhaps I am not "the most," but I have a strong scientific background, enhanced by an approach to life that adds meaning and depth and makes it easier for me to find compassion and understanding for my fellow human beings.

I have spent my life thinking about my experiences, learning from them and trying new ways of communicating with others. My education, experiences, and flexibility make me more able to understand where so many people are coming from. With that understanding, I can write in such a way that people find information and agreement instead of challenge and rejection. Communicating peacefully, I find, helps allay the fears others might have of not being heard, not being understood, and ultimately not being accepted as a human being.

Starting with a childhood that was beyond horrendous, I've lived through many painful things in my life. That, too, helps me understand what people are going through. Through those experiences, I've learned how we can be better able to come through hard times with our hearts and minds and optimism intact.

That's what this book is about: learning how to look at life and our experiences in such a way that we can find peace in our hearts, even if all around us there is no peace. I've written this book from a compassionate and understanding perspective, with the idea that whoever is reading it will appreciate being welcomed and understood, not judged. Many of my early readers have commented that my book is like having a fireside chat with a best friend. I hope you enjoy it and find it valuable.

Marina Michaels
November 1, 2014

Chapter 1

Introduction

From Socrates, we learn that we all have within us the answers to every problem that faces us; we just need to ask ourselves the right questions.

"This man beside us also has a hard fight with an unfavouring world, with strong temptations, with doubts and fears, with wounds of the past which have skinned over, but which smart when they are touched. It is a fact, however surprising. And when this occurs to us, we are moved to deal kindly with him, to bid him be of good cheer, to let him understand that we are also fighting a battle; we are bound not to irritate him, nor press hardly upon him nor help his lower self. "

John Watson, 1903

Whether we know it or not, we all need forgiveness, both to give it and receive it. We may know we aren't forgiving a person or event; we may even want to forgive them. Yet we face seemingly insurmountable barriers. We don't know how to forgive, or why, or where to start. We might have ideas about forgiveness that deter us from wanting to forgive; for example, we might think that a person doesn't deserve to be forgiven, or we might think that forgiving that person means accepting that what they did was all right.

Alternatively, we may not know that we need to forgive. We know we are angry or hurting, but we don't know how to move out of those feelings. We don't know that the solution is to forgive.

And sometimes, surprising though it may seem, we don't always know we are angry or hurting, and so we tell ourselves we are fine and are unaware that we need to forgive.

On top of all that, we often don't know how we can live in such a way that we never take harm or hold onto the pain and anger in the first place, so that forgiveness isn't necessary.

Forgiveness Is a Lifestyle

Forgiveness is something you do within the context of your life, not in isolation from everything else. Like the game of Go, the principles of forgiveness are simple and easy to learn. However, also like the game of Go, these principles can take a lifetime to master. In this book, you'll find information that can help make the process of forgiveness shorter, make it easier for you to forgive people in the future, and learn new ways of thinking so you no longer find yourself responding in unforgiving ways toward others. As you forgive more and more people, and learn to live in a forgiving way, you'll be happier, even healthier, and have more energy to spend on your life in the here-and-now, rather than being stuck in something that happened to you a long time ago. As you do so, your life becomes more loving, more peaceful, and more forgiving.

In short, this book can help you transform your life.

Although this book is unique, and the methods I present are mine, the principles in this book are universal. You can learn everything that is in this book in your own way by being open to new ways of viewing things, paying attention, and thinking about your life.

However, even though you can learn everything that is in this book on your own, the information in this book can accelerate you on your path, so that you move more quickly through troubled and troubling situations. Properly used, the information in this book can be helpful, even transformative. It can bring you new hope—hope that you can start feeling better about yourself and others in your life, and hope that you will be able to forgive more easily now and in the future. And who doesn't want that?

We Have All Been Injured

We all have had experiences that have left us confused, hurt, anguished, sorrowing, angry, bewildered—even filled with rage or despair, or a deep desire for revenge; experiences that have left their mark on us long after the experience ended. By "all," I mean every single human being on this planet. These experiences and their attendant pain are part of being human.

I am no exception. I, too, have experienced a great deal of pain in my life. My childhood was so painful in so many ways that it took years for me to acknowledge the very bad things that happened. I have experienced great loss on many levels—financial and personal; losing someone I've loved; dishonesty and betrayal. And yet, despite everything I've experienced, people often remark on how positive I am and how healthy I seem to be. And I am, but I am not completely unscarred; I am still healing injuries taken in my childhood.

However, I've lived my life in such a way that injuries taken as an adult have not left their mark on me, and I have forgiven those who have injured me. I've had people try to harm me in large ways and small, and have not held on to what was said and done. Some experiences have been easy enough to let go—someone harmed me unintentionally, they apologized (or didn't), and I moved on. Some took work—a little or a lot—to get to the point of forgiveness and that sense of peace in my heart. Some were so painful that I just didn't allow myself to think about them fully until many years after the fact.

Most importantly, using the principles in this book, I forgave my mother many years ago, thankfully (for me) before she died , so it wasn't too late for me to be loving and accepting in her presence, even though she didn't change how she treated me.

I've accomplished this by learning through trial and error how to forgive and how to think about events so that I don't need to forgive, even when bad things happen; in short, how to live a forgiving lifestyle.

Because I have done this, I know that we all can learn how to let go of whatever pain we have experienced, and we can learn how to live in such a way that we don't take harm from such experiences in the future. I believe that we as human beings are striving to become better. We make a lot of mistakes, with ourselves and with each other, in how we think about ourselves and each other, and in what we say and what we do. Many of us learn from the missteps that we take or that the others take. We learn to be better human beings and to stop making those mistakes.

Yet some of us don't. We continue to repeat the same mistakes, make the same types of choices, and experience the same kinds of things. We want to be better, but we don't know how. And although some of us find it easy to forgive, most of us don't, so we hang onto what has happened to us, reliving the pain and anger over and over again.

However, despite whatever challenges we face, we all want peace. We all want to learn to live in harmony and understanding. But we also all have our limitations—our limitations of understanding, our limitations of what we can or are willing to accept.

And that's what this book is about: achieving a greater peace with ourselves, with others, and with the world. As you make changes in your life using the information in this book, you'll learn more about those things that are holding you back from peace. You'll release more of your pain, your anger, your sorrow, your sense of betrayal, and will grow more peaceful and loving in your heart. And as a result, the world you live in will get better.

What To Do About the Pain

Over the years, I've experienced a great deal of pain, and have sometimes had a hard time forgiving those who inflicted it. I am sure you have, too. It doesn't feel good to be hurting, and it feels even worse to continue to feel that pain long after the original harm was done. We experience lingering pain when we can't let go of or forgive what happened or who caused it to happen.

By the very nature of it, we find it hard to get out of that painful place. Sometimes it hurts so much that we don't even allow ourselves to know how much we are hurting, or we don't admit to ourselves that we are hurting at all.

And even if we admit that the pain is there, we often don't know what to do with the pain. We can go to some very dark places where there seems to be no ray of light. We don't know how to let go of the pain, or how to move through it to reach some form of resolution, and we certainly don't know how to forgive the person who inflicted that pain. Sometimes we can arrive at a resolution of sorts, and even achieve some amount of relief. That can take a lifetime and leave much that is painful and unresolved.

But we don't have to just live with the pain, and we don't have to rely on somehow stumbling on the path to wholeness randomly, making many missteps along the way. There are ways by which we can arrive at a better place in regard to something hurtful that has happened to us. The most powerful way to do so is forgiveness.

In this book, I present two methods for forgiveness that I've developed over many years, and a third, preventive approach: a way of living so that you don't hold onto things.

- The first method of forgiveness will sound simple, and it is, but it won't always be easy. However, despite its simplicity, the effects on your life can be deep and permanent.
- The second method is even simpler and definitely easier, but just as effective. However, it can take more time.

You can use either method separately, or you can use both methods together. Some of the benefits of employing either or both of these methods is that, once you have started on the path to forgiveness, it can change your life dramatically for the better.

Sometimes what is causing you pain (or is causing you more pain than it has to) is how you think about and react to a person or event, not the person or situation itself. So the third method in this book isn't directly about forgiveness. You can think of it as a preventive approach, a lifestyle or an approach to life that you can use to prevent having to forgive in the first place. As a powerful complement to the methods of forgiveness described in this book, you'll also find a description of this preventive measure: a collection of guidelines on how to think about what happens to you. This third method gives you information on how you can change the way you think about and react to people and situations from this point forward so that you don't come away from a situation needing to forgive.

In the final chapters of this book, I address special circumstances: forgiving yourself (which could be the hardest task you can take on), forgiving your parents and other family members, and asking for forgiveness from someone you have harmed.

Forgiveness is Possible

When we experience a hurtful situation, in addition to the initial pain and anguish, we can continue to feel pain, anger, bitterness, and resentment long after the event itself is over. We may try to let go of that pain, but we just can't. We keep going over and over what happened, feeling the pain anew each time, perhaps growing angrier or falling more deeply into despair. After a while, it seems as though we will just have to keep living with the pain, thinking that that's just the way things are, and there's nothing that can be done about it.

We might believe that if we forgive the person or people involved, then that means they got away with it. Or we might have tried to forgive the person or people involved, but haven't been able to. We might not know that there are certain prerequisites that must be in place for us to be able to forgive.

The first of those prerequisites is that we must believe that forgiveness is possible. If we don't, we won't even try to forgive, or, if we try, we will give up before we have results. We won't be open to information that can help us, and we will continue to remain in that dark place of pain.

The good news is that the fact that you are reading this book shows that you are open to the possibility of forgiveness, if not in the particular, then in the abstract. I am not asking you to believe right this minute that forgiveness for some particular person or situation is possible. Just keep an open mind about the possibility of forgiveness, and have patience. We'll get there.

Why the Information in this Book Can Work

I have developed the techniques in this book over the years, through trial and error and paying attention to myself and others. Whenever I have decided to apply these techniques, I have been 100 percent successful in forgiving, and in reaching a point of peace in my heart about a particular person or situation.

I say "decided to apply these techniques," with an emphasis on the word "decided," because deciding to forgive is a crucial step. With some situations, we may not be ready to forgive someone, and that's okay. We are all still works in progress. It's important to the forgiveness process that you treat yourself gently and with forgiveness too. If you aren't ready to forgive someone, that's okay; just set them aside for now. (I say more about choosing not to forgive a particular person or situation at the end of Chapter 5.)

While reading this book, you may notice that I've kept it simple and straightforward, focused on meaningful content, with only as many illustrative examples as are helpful. I've done this to make the message of forgiveness palatable and accessible. I want your experience of reading this book to be as pleasant as possible, and I hope you feel safe and welcome.

A Note on Language

The language we use is extremely important. Certain words and terms carry overtones and connotations that influence those listening. The terms you use when speaking about a person will set expectations, affecting how others think about that person. For example, if you say that a person is stubborn, that will affect how other people think about and react to that person. It colors how they interpret that other person's words and actions. If you instead say that the same person sticks to their principles, that also affects how others think about that person, but in a somewhat more positive way.

Because language is important, throughout this book, I have used language that is accepting, forgiving, and allowing, while also encouraging responsibility.

Chapter 2

We Are Living in Pain

How does a lack of forgiveness affect our health and our relationships? Why are we not forgiving? Why can't we let go? Why should we let go?

"Anger is an acid that can do more harm to the vessel in which it is stored than to anything on which it is poured."
Mark Twain

We have all had things happen to us. Bad things. Hurtful things. Things that caused us to feel angry, anguished, bitter, and resentful; we might even feel hatred. Sometimes we have been able to move on from those events without taking damage or continuing to feel the pain; other times, those things left us feeling scarred and incomplete, perhaps even feeling we are broken and can never be healed. And sometimes we have continued holding our pain against someone or something, blaming them for what happened, not forgiving them, but instead feeling those same feelings, thinking those same thoughts, every time we think of the person or situation.

In addition to feeling that pain from not forgiving, we often want to correct people, to show them how wrong they are, and sometimes even to get revenge. None of those desires and feelings can feel good, nor are they conducive to good relationships. If we don't forgive, if we don't let go of those thoughts and feelings, and if we make a habit of unforgivingness, then we accumulate poison in our hearts.

The Harm Done

When we aren't forgiving someone or some event or situation, even though we try not to think of that person, we can't always help it, and when we think of that person, we feel angry all over again, either at that person for what he/she did, or at ourselves for allowing it to happen. Or both. It preys on our minds and sense of peace and well-being. It also affects our health.

Anger, a common emotion when we aren't forgiving someone, isn't necessarily bad (because it can alert us that something is wrong that needs to be addressed). Yet if we don't act on anger constructively, especially if we are habitually angry, it can cause us physical harm. Frequent anger takes a toll on our bodies, taxing our nervous systems and our hearts, liver, and kidneys, greatly increasing the risk of heart problems, and ultimately decreasing our life expectancy. And meanwhile, it is hard to be happy or to enjoy life when we are angry.

Resentment and bitterness can affect our health in the same ways as anger, leading to heart disease, affecting our immune systems, and contributing to a host of other bodily ills, such as headaches, backaches, fatigue, and arthritis. When we aren't forgiving someone, we are holding onto emotions and habits of thought that cause those ills.

The Desire for Revenge

As Commander Shepherd in *Mass Effect 2* says, "You're endangering lives—and the mission—for your own selfish revenge." Revenge is damaging to yourself and others. The desire to get revenge is hard to overcome, because often that desire for revenge is a habitual response to being deeply hurt or to someone close to us being deeply hurt. (And also because the desire for revenge, by its very nature, arises out of blaming someone else rather than accepting responsibility for our thoughts and reactions.) Sometimes we want revenge because we (or someone we love) was badly hurt, and we want to see justice done, or we want to lash out and hurt that other person as badly as they hurt us (or ours).

Other times our desire for revenge is because we experienced a minor slight, or someone did something that was part of their job, or something happened that arose out of a normal human interaction, and we blew it out of proportion. Maybe whatever happened inconvenienced us, or caused us to lose face, and we don't know of any other way to deal with it than to respond with the desire to crush that person.

If this describes you, if you want to be happier, and to have happier relationships, and to stop causing harm to others, then one big step toward greater harmony would be to learn to let go, to forgive, and to view things differently. It can be helpful to use the principles and approaches described in Chapter 4 for changing your thinking.

Our Emotional Well-Being Is Affected

In addition to affecting us physically, lack of forgiveness and its attendant pain affects our well-being. It holds us back from feeling completely happy, whole, and in the moment. It keeps us hostage in a past filled with confusion, pain, and anger. It keeps us focused on what is wrong in our lives rather than what is right. It keeps us from moving forward into new, healthier, happier experiences. Because it affects our attitude and outlook, it can poison the relationships we have now, because it is hard for others to have a good relationship with us if we are focused on our pain, whether that pain is anger, resentment, or something else. It can keep us from getting close to others because we fear that others will do the same thing to us that was done to us in the past. And, insidiously, it can keep us from realizing just how much we are in charge of our thoughts and our reactions.

But I don't believe that anyone truly wants to be in that place of pain, anger, resentment, and blame. It doesn't feel good or right; it clashes with our innate sense that things can and should be better, even if we cover up that sense with thoughts some have taught us to think of as being more "realistic." We've all heard these mantras:

- people can't change
- life isn't fair

- bad things happen for no reason
- you can't be truly happy in this vale of tears we call life—so whatever has happened to you, you might as well deal with it. And by "deal with it," people usually mean "accept that you are hurt and live with the fact that that isn't going to change."

But I believe that there is a different way to look at things. You can take certain steps, steps that I describe later in this book, to accept your pain, examine it, learn what is helpful to learn from it, and then release it, transforming it into something that strengthens you and warms you and gives you greater courage and skill to deal with pain in the future.

Denial is a Dead End

Although we all want to be whole and free of pain, sometimes the pain is so bad that we shy away from it, pretending it doesn't exist. But as long as we pretend something doesn't exist, we are not dealing with it. This is denial. Denial may keep us from realizing we are in pain, but the pain is still there, and that pain deeply affects us and our relationships. If we don't deal with it, we can never be whole. Accepting that something happened and that you experienced pain is a good first step toward that wholeness.

In a way, denial is like an anesthetic—whatever is causing the pain is still happening, and our bodies are still experiencing the trauma, but the messages aren't getting to our conscious awareness. Denial as a first response to a hurtful situation can be helpful because it gives us breathing room in which to come to terms with what happened. But if carried on too long, denial prevents us from dealing with the pain. Denial doesn't fix the problem; it only makes it seem less urgent, but the hurt is still there.

Let's take a look at the forms denial takes, and why we deny.

Four Forms of Denial, or Why We Can't Let Go

We deal with such emotions as anger, fear, and resentment in different ways. Here are four forms that denial typically takes. They aren't exclusive of each other; we might employ two of more of these forms for the same situation. As long as we are in denial, we won't be able to move on to the next step in healing and forgiving.

Sometimes we direct those emotions at a person, group, or situation that we feel wronged us or harmed us, blaming them for whatever caused us to feel that way. This is denial of our responsibility.

Sometimes we pretend we aren't feeling the way we are feeling. This is denial of our feelings.

Sometimes we make excuses for the people involved, belittling our own pain. This is denial of our own experience.

And sometimes we allow ourselves to wallow in the pain, using the pain itself as an excuse to never heal. This is denial of our ability to move beyond.

Directing blame at others is denial because we are saying that we have nothing to do with the situation; we have no responsibility or accountability for it. By saying we have no responsibility for the situation, we are also saying we have no way to resolve it. The truth is that we always have choices, no matter what the situation, and those choices include how we think about and respond to a situation and other people.

Of course, it is also denial to pretend that those emotions aren't there, or pretend that whatever happened was okay or that we weren't really as hurt by it as we truly have been. We hide from ourselves the fact that we are hurting or angry. When people say to us, "You sound pretty angry about that," or comment upon how hurtful a situation must have been, we say, in what we think is all honesty, that no, we aren't angry or hurt.

A more insidious form of denial comes when we acknowledge that we are angry or hurt, but we tell ourselves that whoever did that to us was doing the best they could in the circumstances. This might sometimes be the truth, but sometimes isn't, and anyway is unhelpful in terms of relieving our pain. We do this because we are reluctant to think that someone might have deliberately hurt us, and we hope that it will somehow make it all right if we can just convince ourselves that the person did everything he or she could. Taking this approach also belittles our own pain, and is another way by which we further hurt ourselves.

The fourth form of denial we might take is to just wallow in the pain without doing anything about it, repeatedly going over the situation in our minds, feeling the pain again and again, maybe even finding new ways in which we are hurt by whatever happened. While we do this, we tell ourselves that, although we want out of the pain, there is no way to get out of it. Or we argue with ourselves and others about how our pain and our circumstances are special and different from anything anyone else is experiencing; that our situation is extraordinary and unique, and particularly tough. In that way we can paint ourselves as the heroes in our own tragic story. Noble but doomed, we suffer, and let everyone around us know we are suffering. But because we have convinced ourselves that there is nothing that can be done to make things better, we reject any attempts to help us.

When we choose to deny our pain and responsibility to ourselves in any of these ways, we can't forgive the situation, nor can we move beyond it. We only continue to perpetuate it by holding onto those feelings and not working through them. We are stuck in a bad, hurting place in our hearts. Deep down, we want to get out of that place, to be released from the pain, but we have never truly had any hope that such a release is possible. We can't let go of the pain because we are in denial about our ability to deal with it.

Denial keeps us in a cycle of repeating the same kinds of experiences. But why do we repeat them? Because we repeatedly put ourselves into situations that give us the opportunity to heal ourselves. What do I mean by that? I mean we recreate situations that are similar to a prior situation in which we had been hurt, a situation during which we made certain decisions about ourselves and others. We recreate this experiences so we can make different choices and decisions. In making those different decisions, we can achieve different outcomes. However, denial prevents us from learning from those experiences, and therefore from healing through what we could have learned from them.

As a greatly simplified example, if we had a domineering parent who belittled us, we often get into relationships with significant others who are domineering and belittling, which gives us the opportunity to heal that original wound by making different decisions about ourselves and others. (Though we often don't heal that wound, because we focus on the "what" of the here and now rather than trying to understand the why.)

Denial only gets us more of the same kinds of experiences because, although we are in a situation, we aren't dealing with it, and therefore we aren't making new, wiser, healthier choices. Until we face what happened and heal the underlying cause (the original cause being our set of initial choices and decisions), we'll just keep on hurting ourselves.

Hanging Onto Pain

When people do things to us that we don't forgive, our lack of forgiveness affects us far more strongly that it ever will affect them.

Although holding onto pain is not going to heal us, it is better than denying it. If we admit that the pain is there, we can move on to the next step, which is thinking it through so we can arrive at a resolution, which brings healing. But when we take this next step, we don't have to rely on somehow stumbling on the path to wholeness randomly, making many mis-steps along the way. There is so much more to life, so much more that is wonderful—joy, love, contentment, happiness, and peace. Those things are all there to be had no matter what our life circumstances, but we won't see our way there until we start to believe in them. And one way we can start to believe in them is through forgiveness.

Why We Hold On

Why do we hold onto our pain? Because we are afraid. Aside from not knowing or believing that there is a solution, fundamentally, we hold on to our pain because we are afraid of our thoughts and emotions, and we are trying to avoid fully facing them.

Like water, our feelings stagnate when they are confined, and are healthiest when they are allowed to move. What do I mean by "allowing feelings to move"? It means admitting to ourselves that those feelings are present, and allowing ourselves to feel everything, and not to pretend to ourselves that we are not feeling them (such as allowing ourselves to acknowledge that we are feeling angry).

During the process of allowing ourselves to feel everything, our thoughts and emotions will transform and transmute, taking us on a journey of awareness and healing. Fully and healthily expressed, any emotion can bring us to a peaceful place. ("Healthily expressed" is important—expressing or acting out our emotions in an unhealthy manner will not bring us to a peaceful place, and can even do harm to ourselves and others.)

Fear Can Block Us

The thought of allowing ourselves to feel our emotions—to acknowledge them and to truly look at them—can be frightening. Some feelings are very hard to face, especially the darker ones. It is hard to admit we are feeling anger, even rage, toward someone; harder still to allow ourselves to fully feel that anger. Sometimes we are afraid of what we might do if we allow ourselves to feel those emotions. We are afraid we might do harm to someone. Other times we are afraid we can't handle these feelings. We are afraid we might implode or explode, or that we will break down, or harm ourselves, or withdraw from life.

However, often our fear makes what we fear increase in size and seem insurmountable or unfaceable. We must face our fear, or it will ruin our lives. By its nature, fear makes it hard to face what we fear. In facing our fears, the thing we feared can diminish and become manageable. We also feel a lot better about ourselves when we face our fears.

Here's an example. Long ago, I was experiencing a series of nightmares from which I woke in terror, heart pounding, body frozen in fear. After a few years of these nightmares, I read that the best way to handle such nightmares is to, within the dream, face whatever is frightening you and say that it can't hurt you. So one night, during one of these nightmares, I remembered those words of advice. I stopped running, turned to face the nightmare thing that was chasing me, and said, "You can't hurt me." As soon as I said those words, I realized their truth, and the thing that was chasing me transformed. No longer a malevolent, sentient presence, it became a harmless wind that passed me by.

Our waking fears can be faced like that as well. The thing we have been avoiding, that has grown into an overwhelming obstacle in our minds, can become harmless and small once we actually face it. This is especially true about facing the fears and hurt and anger and other feelings that we experience when thinking about a person or situation.

But fear won't go away by itself. You can't just tell yourself that you will do something once you stop being afraid of doing it. You must make the first step out of fear while you are still afraid.

Acknowledging that we are afraid, and acknowledging what we are afraid of, is that first step.

When we acknowledge that those feelings are there and start looking at them, then our emotions will start flowing, moving, and changing. When denied and unexpressed, the darker emotions, such as anger, can't change; they can only fester. Once allowed out into the light of our more fully conscious awareness, they start to become healthier. They can also transmute into something else—even joy and relief, as the process we go through when looking at those emotions brings the understanding that we had been missing.

Expressing our emotions healthily is key to the forgiveness process. It is unhealthy to blame others for our feelings, or to use our emotions as an excuse to attack someone or try to harm them in turn (including ourselves). Just because we are angry doesn't mean we have the right to take that out on anyone, either the person we are angry with or anyone else. The healthy expression of an emotion involves allowing ourselves to feel that emotion in a safe place and manner. That often means writing it down in a diary, or shouting it out (in a quiet place where no one can hear us), or talking it over with someone we trust (such as a counselor or a friend we completely trust to listen to what we have to say without trying to interject his or her own opinions and without telling anyone else about it), or perhaps taking some constructive physical action, such as taking a walk.

But it isn't just fear of our emotions that can hold us back, keeping us from forgiving. Sometimes we are so hurt or angry that we are unwilling to let go of those feelings toward another person. Sometimes we just don't want to forgive them. And somehow we think we are getting even with them or punishing them by holding on that way.

We Want to Be Right

Why is that? How is it that we think we're punishing the other person by not forgiving them? Are we thinking that somehow we are having an effect on them? Are they even in our lives anymore? Do they know how we are feeling? Will they ever know? Do they care?

The bottom line is that holding onto such feelings as resentment, anger, blame, doubt, and fear doesn't affect those other people. We are the ones holding onto those feelings and thinking those thoughts. We are the ones being affected by our unwillingness to forgive, not the other person. And deep down inside, we know this truth. Yet we persist in holding onto those feelings and thoughts. We find it hard to let go.

One reason for this is that fundamentally, everyone, each person, you and I, wants to be right. Being wrong shakes our confidence and threatens our survival. When someone does something we disagree with, we want to think that the other person is wrong; we don't want to think that perhaps we and they can both be right. Also, we don't want to feel we were wrong about judging a person or situation, or about having taken harm from it.

If someone does something contrary to what we think is right, and it causes harm, some of us feel particularly angry that we haven't been listened to, especially when the result was that someone (ourselves or someone else) got hurt. In those cases, our natural inclination is to turn on the person who didn't listen and to attack them, even if only mentally, to punish them for being wrong.

Other times we stonewall, shutting down and not confronting the situation, with the idea that that shows them how wrong they are. More perniciously, sometimes we roll over and expose the white throat of surrender to that person, mentally and emotionally opening ourselves up to more harm. We think that somehow we deserved the harm that was done, and that if only we show them how vulnerable we are, or if only we tell them that they were right and we were wrong, they will stop harming us. We might tell ourselves that if only we love them enough, they will change and stop hurting us.

All of these responses can get in the way of healing and forgiving.

We Don't Know How To Let Go

Another reason for holding on is that we don't know how to let go. We don't know how to stop feeling those feelings and thinking those thoughts. We don't understand what happened, or how it happened, or how someone could have done something that was so hurtful. We believe that they must have done it on purpose, and we don't understand how someone could deliberately cause pain like that. Out of our lack of understanding, we hold it against them that they were willing and able to hurt us.

The truth is that sometimes, out of ignorance or a lack of understanding on their part, or out of carelessness and recklessness, people cause harm and hurt others without meaning to. Some people just don't understand other people who are different from them, and out of their lack of understanding, they thoughtlessly do or say things that hurt. They might even think they are doing something positive and are bewildered when it backfires. Or they are irresponsible and drive while under the influence of some drug (including alcohol).

They don't mean to do the harm that results when they lose control of their vehicle, but they do harm anyway, and that's hard to forgive because we think that everybody knows better than to drive while under the influence.

Now, I am not saying that nobody ever does anything deliberately harmful, because some people do. Some people deliberately try to hurt others. These are not good people. But that doesn't mean that you have to hold onto the harm they inflicted by not forgiving the situation. In fact, by holding onto the hurt or anger, you are allowing their actions to continue to hurt you. In doing so, you are continuing to hurt yourself. It's as though they stabbed you once, and you keep picking at the wound so it doesn't have a chance to heal. If you can come to an understanding about this kind of person and the situation you were in with them, that wound will have a chance to close and to heal.

Letting Go Can Be Hard

Letting go can be hard, especially if we have certain ideas about how something should be done, and someone else has violated those ideas. There's a parable about two monks that illustrates this principle.

Two monks had vowed never to touch a woman. One day, as they were traveling by foot through a mountainous region, they came to a river with no bridge. The only suitable area for fording the river was rocky and deep, with strong, swift-flowing waters. A small, frail old woman was standing at the ford, unable to cross. When the monk arrived, she cried out in relief.

"Good monks, can one of you please carry me across this stream? I am old and my footing is uncertain."

The first monk refused self-righteously, but the other calmly picked her up, carried her on his back across the stream, then put her down safely on the other side.

After accepting her thanks, the monks continued on in silence, mile after mile. But the more the first monk thought about the scene at the ford, the angrier he became. Finally, he just couldn't stand it any longer. He burst out, berating his companion, saying, "How could you touch her? We made sacred vows! It's just terrible what you did. How can you live with yourself? You're a disgrace!"

To which the second monk mildly replied, "I set that woman down miles ago. You're still carrying her."

Sometimes when we continue to be angry at someone, it is because of our own ways of thinking about what they did. We just can't let go of the situation or the fact that they did something we don't agree with; perhaps that we don't understand.

You've Tried Forgiving Before, But It Didn't Work

So that's the problem: we have had something bad happen to us, or a lot of bad things, hurting us beyond measure, and we can't let go of the pain. We can't forgive the situation or the person or people responsible. The pain is affecting our lives in many ways, including our physical and emotional health. Most of us know that hanging onto these feelings is harmful or at least uncomfortable, but we don't know what to do.

Forgiveness is an integral part of healing and wholeness. There are many conscious, deliberate ways by which we can arrive at forgiveness and understanding in regard to something that has happened to us. Yet although some of us have tried to forgive, perhaps trying a specific method, we just didn't get results. Why is that? Why don't we get results?

One reason could be that the methods we've tried just weren't for us. Not everyone's method is right for everyone. The well-known family counselor, Virginia Satir, reportedly once said that, in all her years of counseling, she had learned that there are 265 ways to wash the dishes, and every method gets the dishes clean. One person's method for reaching forgiveness may work for some people, but it might not work for others.

Another reason could be that perhaps there was something inaccessible to us in the way the person writing about that method said it; we might have had a hard time "getting" what they had to say, or it just didn't resonate with something for us. This is nothing against either us or the person presenting the method. How each person communicates is unique, even if they are saying the same thing as someone else, but in a different way. Sometimes it is easier to hear and understand a message when one person says it, than it is to hear the same message when another person says it.

If you've tried forgiving before, and it didn't work for you, please don't give up on the thought that you can forgive. It is a fact about we humans that when we follow instructions and don't get the expected results, our most common reaction is to blame ourselves rather than think perhaps the method (or the way it was explained) just isn't working for us. So when we don't get results, we think we, not the method, are at fault. As a result, we may give up on trying to make any improvements in our lives in that area. We may even lose faith in the possibility of making progress. At best, we move on to try something else, often with the same unsatisfying results, and still end up blaming ourselves. It just doesn't occur to most of us to think that perhaps the method just wasn't the right tool for us, or the way the method was communicated just didn't explain it well enough to us. None of us are "one size fits all"; we are all unique. There are some methods that work well for some people, and other methods that work well for others. Some ways of writing are crystal clear for some people, but not for everyone.

I believe that if you follow the advice and methods in this book, you will find yourself able to forgive others and yourself, first in small ways, and then in larger ones. Because of this, your outlook will be more positive, you'll be happier and healthier, and your life will be better. However, although I have used the methods in this book with great success, I fully understand that you might not like my approaches, or they might not resonate with you or that you might have a hard time understanding what I am trying to explain. As my friend, Karen Marshall, said about forgiveness, "It's such a personal topic, you have to find someone on your wavelength [to speak to you about it]."

If I'm not on your wavelength, then please don't give up on learning how to forgive, and please don't blame yourself for not getting anything from this book; just find someone who does speak to you in a way that is accessible and understandable. I encourage you to keep looking because this book is about forgiveness, and that includes forgiving yourself, and not blaming yourself.

In short, give the information and methods in this book a try, but if they don't work for you, stay positive about your ability to forgive and keep looking for information on the topic.

Chapter 3

But We Don't Have To

No matter how hard you think it might be, it is possible to forgive. Learn five powerful reasons to forgive, what forgiveness is (and isn't), and why you don't always have to forgive.

"When you hold resentment toward another, you are bound to that person or condition by an emotional link that is stronger than steel. Forgiveness is the only way to dissolve that link and get free."
Katherine Ponder

Forgiveness is for your own sake. When we haven't forgiven someone or let go of a situation, we suffer, experiencing such things as anger, resentment, blame, or sorrow. As described in Chapter 2, lack of forgiveness affects us physically and emotionally.

The solution to our pain is forgiveness. Forgiveness frees us from that suffering, frees us from the thoughts and feelings we've been having about that person or situation. Forgiveness is for us. It has little or nothing to do with whoever it is we aren't forgiving.

Five Powerful Reasons To Forgive

Perhaps you don't need to be convinced that forgiveness is a good thing. But if you do need convincing, here are five powerful reasons why it is good to forgive.

Reason 1: Released Pain

The first powerful reason is that when we forgive, we release pain we have been carrying around with us for a long time. Sometimes it is terrible pain, and sometimes not so terrible, but it is pain nonetheless. When we forgive, it is pain we no longer need to carry. Sometimes we aren't even aware of how much we were hurting until we release that pain; releasing that pain can make us feel so much better.

Reason 2: Improved Relationships

The second powerful reason is that as we release the pain, we improve our relationships. When we are not forgiving someone, we are feeling pain, bitterness, anger, despair, anguish, and resentment. All those feelings and their associated thoughts can consume our lives, affecting our physical, mental, and emotional health, and also affecting our relationships with others. Nobody enjoys watching a loved one suffer constantly, nor is it easy being around someone who is chronically angry, sad, or resentful, and yet that is what we are putting our family, friends, and coworkers through when we can't or won't let go of a painful situation. What is more, when we are suffering, we cannot be the best we can be for ourselves and those around us. Getting out of that state and into a better one is a good reason to forgive.

Reason 3: The Ripple Effect

The third powerful reason to forgive is the double ripple effect of starting the process of forgiveness. The first ripple effect is this: as you touch one emotional sore spot and start to heal it, you'll find that other, related sore spots also start to heal in surprising ways, sometimes seemingly without effort. Your heart will be lighter, your outlook brighter, and your energy renewed. The second ripple effect is this: when you relate in new and more forgiving ways with others, you affect their lives positively, and they in turn affect the lives of others positively, and so on. You may find that you attract new people into your life who are more positive and pleasant to be with.

Reason 4: The Synergistic Effect

The fourth powerful reason is that, as you forgive one person or situation, you'll find it easier to forgive another, compounding the positive effects in your life.

Reason 5: Healing and Transcendence

The fifth powerful reason to forgive is that forgiving someone can have immense healing power and even affect you spiritually. By illustration, I'll share an experience I had years ago.

Long ago, I was married to a man who neither loved nor respected me. He showed that lack of love and respect in many different ways. Although I suspected it, and tried to talk with him about it, he never admitted it, and he instead continued to do and say unloving things. We had a young daughter who adored him and whom he adored, and I didn't want to consider divorce, but I was miserable. I felt unloved and was angry and unhappy. To complicate matters, we had very different ideas of how to raise our daughter. We fought a lot, not in a healthy or loving way, which was bad for our daughter to see, and I kept focusing on everything he was doing that was wrong.

Things eventually got to the point where I could see no happiness for any of us if I stayed. So I decided to divorce him, but because of my belief in resolving things in my heart before moving on, I felt it would be best to work through in my heart and mind what had been going on in our marriage, accept responsibility for my part in it, and forgive him for everything he had done. The first step I needed to take was to find willingness in my heart to forgive him, and that's where I hit a snag in my plan. I just could not bring myself to be willing to forgive him.

I struggled for weeks with that unwillingness. During that time, I asked myself a lot of hard questions (and got a lot of hard answers), thought about my reasons for being unwilling, and worked through a lot of pain and frustration. I argued with myself a lot, trying to exclude aspects of the situation from my plan of forgiveness, telling myself that some things were unforgivable and that he was just plain wrong, so why should I forgive him? I just couldn't find myself willing to forgive him.

Then one night I had a dream about him that helped bring clarity to the situation; a dream that gave me a new way of looking at him and our relationship. When I woke up, I found that I was able to decide that I was willing to let him be who he was, just as he was, and not continue to hold anything against him. In making this decision, I held nothing back. I was completely willing to let him be himself, however much I disagreed with his methods or approach.

And with that decision, a huge wave of love and acceptance came pouring through my heart. It was a physical sensation like none I had ever felt before—a clear, clean flow of unconditional love stronger than any love I had ever felt. It was like pure light.

That light shone on everything: everything my then-husband had done, and everything he or anyone else had done to me. While the light poured through, it shone on everything he continued to do. It didn't change what he was doing, or what anyone else was doing, it just changed how I felt about it. That light kept pouring through my heart for six months. Nothing bothered me during that time. And even after the light faded, the anger and resentment over those past events did not return. It felt so good to finally let go of the feelings I had been carrying around with me about that situation.

This experience was such a revelation to me. I realized how important willingness is, and I decided to learn how to forgive. I started experimenting with different methods. I admit I didn't read much about it, and this was in the early days of the Internet, so the wonderful resources available now were not available then. Instead, I decided to trust my intelligence and common sense and let those two guide me. It took a number of years of thinking of and testing different approaches, but eventually I developed the methods I describe in this book, and have used them to good effect many times.

Not everyone will have such dramatic results when they decide to be willing to forgive someone, but every time you do decide to be willing, and every time you forgive someone to any extent, you will experience emotional healing and gain increased wholeness in your life. The effects will be permanent and cumulative.

However, and this is very important: forgiving someone releases you from the pain of not forgiving. It frees you of the anger, resentment, blame, and other feelings that you are experiencing because you aren't forgiving someone. However, it doesn't always heal the harm they did to you. For example, if you experienced a great deal of abuse as a child, so that you have come to believe that you are not worth much as a human being, then forgiving your parents won't necessarily change that belief. It will, however, help you clear out a lot of the emotional pain so that you will be able to tackle that false belief about yourself.

It Is Within Your Capabilities to Forgive

You may be telling yourself that mine is an extraordinary case, and that your situation is different. You may think yourself incapable of forgiving, or that forgiveness is too hard. But it is within your capabilities to forgive. How long it takes will vary, but you will eventually be able to forgive even the worst hurt. We are all in a process of becoming more than what we were. Some of us move more quickly than others, but we are all on the path.

A wise man once told me that, when trying to reach a solution with someone, as soon as you say a solution can't be found, you make it impossible to find a solution (for one reason, because you stop trying). But as long as you maintain an optimistic attitude, and tell yourself and the other party that a solution can and will be found, you are much more likely to find that solution.

The same is true for forgiveness. As long as you tell yourself that you can't forgive, you won't be able to forgive. If you keep an open mind and allow for the possibility that you can forgive even the hardest situations, then you are much more likely to do so.

It Is Never Too Late

We've all done things that we regret. We've all had things done to us that perhaps others regret, whether they acknowledged it or not, whether they conveyed those regrets to us or not. And to a certain extent, regret can help us by preventing us from doing that same thing again. Those who may have done harm to us may have learned from their actions and may have never done harm in that way again to anyone else.

Forgiveness is for our own sakes. If you have held onto something for a long time, you may be feeling it is too late to start forgiving now. You might be asking yourself, "What good will it do?" Or, "There is so much to forgive; how can I even start?" That's what this book is about.

But it is never too late to forgive. Setting aside thoughts of time being non-linear (that's a completely different book), the past is in the past. You can't do anything about what you have or haven't done. And the future is not yet here; so it isn't set in stone. But you are alive now, and you can do anything in this moment. If something has happened that is continuing to bother you, then you can deal with it in this moment. In doing so, you will be able to move those emotions and lighten your load, emotionally, mentally, and physically speaking, thereby developing a more positive and optimistic outlook. And the more positive and optimistic you become, the healthier you can be.

What Is Forgiveness?

What is forgiveness? Forgiveness means different things to different people, so it is hard to come up with one definition that can satisfy everyone. However, for many people, three major stumbling blocks to forgiveness are

- The belief that forgiveness means condoning what was done. It doesn't.
- The belief that if we forgive, that means our feelings aren't valid. They are.
- The belief that forgiving someone means we were wrong in taking harm. We weren't.

What forgiveness does mean is arriving at a sense of peace in our minds and hearts about a person or situation. It means releasing ourselves from such feelings as anger, shame, anguish, bitterness, blame, resentment, and fear. It means releasing everyone involved, including ourselves, from the prison in our minds or hearts that we keep them in. It means improving our health as we are able to release and change harmful thoughts and feelings. It means improving our relationships, now and for the future.

In the majority of cases, when we aren't forgiving someone, the other person involved isn't even aware of how you are feeling, or perhaps doesn't care how you are feeling, or (horribly) would be very happy knowing that you are suffering. (I say, "in the majority of cases," because sometimes it is a family member you are holding your lack of forgiveness against. Family members almost certainly are aware of how you are feeling, and care about it one way or another. You'll find more on forgiving family members in Chapter 12.)

In any case, it doesn't matter what the other person or persons think or feel about the situation. What matters is what you think and what you are feeling.

Forgiveness is Redemption and Healing

At the core, forgiveness is about love, acceptance, and redemption—redemption for yourself, and redemption in your heart for other people. The relief you feel when you finally release all those thoughts and feelings is worth the time and effort it takes to forgive.

Forgiveness and unforgiveness are both judgments and decisions you have made about a person, place, group, or event, including (and especially) yourself. You have either decided to accept whatever happened and not let it ruin your life, or you have decided that whatever happened is something that you can never let go of; that whoever did that thing doesn't deserve your forgiveness.

But everyone deserves forgiveness. When you believe that someone is unforgivable, then you are saying they cannot be redeemed. And as soon as you say that one person is unforgivable, you open the way to saying that others are unforgivable. Ultimately, you are saying that you, too, could be unforgivable.

This is one of the truths of forgiveness: either we are all forgivable, or none of us are.

If you want to look at it from a religious perspective, our creators are not limited in their ability to forgive, and neither are you.

In short, forgiveness isn't for other people; it is for you. You are redeeming yourself. You are rescuing yourself from a self-constructed prison of anger, hatred, resentment, regrets, sorrow, and pain.

As you go through the process of forgiveness, you'll find that everything changes. Your life will change as you practice the techniques in this book with willingness, with honesty, with trust, and with gratitude. These things couldn't help but change your life anyway, but combined with forgiving yourself and others, they will make deep, powerful, and permanent changes in your soul.

Forgiveness Doesn't Change Others

Forgiving someone doesn't change the person you are forgiving; it changes you. For example, if someone is abusing you, or has abused you, forgiving them won't change them. As a corollary, you don't have to accept that abuse. Separate the person from the action, and forgive the person, but don't keep accepting the action. Even though the action wasn't okay, you can still find forgiveness for the person.

Forgiving someone doesn't mean you have to stay in a relationship with that person; the process of forgiveness might also involve realizing that the harm and abuse will continue as long as you stick around, so you might have to distance yourself from that person.

In this way, forgiveness is also about learning to love yourself enough to insist on being treated lovingly, and not sacrificing yourself on the altar of someone else's need to harm others.

You Don't Always Need to Forgive

You don't always need to forgive, nor can anything in the world force you to.

"So what's the deal?" you ask. "You've told me all the reasons why forgiveness is important, and now you are telling me that I don't need to forgive. Why?"

The deal is, your life will be better if you forgive. In your willingness to forgive, your heart expands. And as you forgive, life expands around you.

However, you are never under any obligation—except to yourself—to forgive. When I say "to yourself," I mean that you owe it to yourself to become as healthy and whole and free as you can, and lack of forgiveness stands in the way of that duty to yourself. Yet sometimes you aren't ready to forgive. If you aren't ready to forgive, pressuring yourself to forgive would be counterproductive.

However, it is unusual that someone is unwilling to forgive everyone and everything all at once. It is more likely that you might be ready to forgive some people or situations, but you are not ready to forgive others. So as you apply yourself to forgiving, keep in mind that you don't have to forgive everyone at once. You can hold some people or situations in reserve for a later time when you are more ready to forgive them.

It also might be helpful to remember that forgiveness won't necessarily come all at once. You might be able to forgive everything about a person or situation all at once, but you might also find that you need more time with certain parts of it. You might be able to let go of some feelings, but not others. This is okay. Whatever progress you make in forgiveness, that's progress toward healing and wholeness. Even if it takes years for you to forgive someone, that's okay.

The important thing when you are working on forgiving someone is that you are doing that work and that you are willing to move your heart in a more generous, loving, and forgiving direction in regard to him or her.

Chapter 4

The Nine Principles of the Forgiving Lifestyle

Forgiveness alone isn't enough. If we want to live in such a way that we don't need to forgive, we need to adopt certain ways of thinking and acting. Learn about nine principles that, if followed, will make your life easier, happier, more pleasant, and less filled with conflict.

We are what we repeatedly do. Excellence,
then, is not an act, but a habit.
Aristotle, Nicomachean Ethics

Forgiveness is not an occasional act,
it is a constant attitude.
Martin Luther King

Wouldn't it be great if, when something potentially harmful happens, something that the old you would have resented and held onto for a long time, you are instead able to live through it and come out unscathed and even happy? Or, if not happy, then at least grateful for the experience? Or even better, to not even be touched by the harm others are trying to do? That state of being is entirely possible and within anyone's reach.

As Shakespeare said, "There is nothing either good or bad, but thinking makes it so" (Hamlet, Act 2, Scene 2). It all boils down to the way we think about what happens to us, not just in the moment that it is happening, but also later. That way of thinking affects how we respond to that situation and whether we carry that situation with us long after the situation is over.

How we think affects everything in our lives, including our relationships with our friends, family, and coworkers. This applies to both how we think about ourselves, and how we think about others. It affects how we interpret what others are doing. If we are habitually suspicious or take offense easily, then we will feel that life or other people are getting the better of us; that we are put upon; that we can't trust anyone. We may see harm where none was intended, or react defensively to something that wasn't meant to be a threat. We will view everything that happens to us in a negative light, and will always be adding to our list of people we are not at peace with, people we dislike or even hate, people we want to take revenge upon. Or, we will always be feeling like we can never get ahead or have anything good happen to us.

How we think also affects how we treat others—what we say and how we say it. For good or ill, our thoughts and feelings are evident in our tone of voice, our facial expressions, and our body language. If we are suspicious or angry or resentful, it shows.

At some point we all realize this isn't winning us any friends or making our lives more peaceful. Sometimes we think we've gone too far down a certain road to ever change direction. But it is never too late. We can change how we think and how we feel about ourselves and others. We can change what we are doing and how we are doing it. In doing so, we change ourselves and our relationships so that we are happier and freer of anger, resentment, and other such feelings. Those changes might be too late to salvage some relationships, but they will salvage others, and will make our new relationships happier, closer, warmer, and more rewarding.

Because how we think is fundamental to how we perceive our world, in changing our thinking, we will change how we perceive the world. We will no longer dwell in that dark valley of resentment, bitterness, pain, and anger. When, as part of that change, we forgive, and develop a forgiving nature, we wash our hearts clean of the anger, the sadness, the resentment, and the other poisons we've accumulated, and we free our bodies and minds of the constant stresses of being unforgiving and of habitually taking harm, and we improve our relationships with ourselves, with others, and with the world.

In order to be able to make this change, in addition to forgiving as described in Chapter 8, we also need to change some habits of thinking and develop specific ways of dealing with life's events as they happen so that we think about and respond to those events differently, as described in this chapter.

Our Thoughts and Our Responses Are Our Choice

We have all seen someone come through a difficult experience unscathed, an experience to which we say, "How could that person possibly forgive what happened?" The "how" is that that person didn't take offense in the first place, and also thought about the situation in a way that made it possible for that person to come through the situation intact. Others might argue that it is just in that person's nature not to take offense, and that other, more normal human beings would be justified in feeling angry, or bitter, or resentful.

There is some truth to the idea that it can be in some people's nature not to take offense, but it isn't just in their nature. It is also how they think about the situation they're in, and how they choose to respond to it. They might not always have been like that; they might have learned a way of thinking and responding that makes them happier.

If you are thinking that it isn't possible to change in this way, then consider this: no one is in charge of your mind except you. No one can make choices for you that you don't agree to. You are in control of how you think and the choices you make. It has nothing to do with the type of person you are; whoever you are, only you can think your thoughts and make your choices.

I've used the principles in this chapter to live through many situations without retaining any anger or bitterness about those situations or the people involved; in other words, without having the need to forgive. So much depends on your thinking.

There are different ways of thinking about anything, and there are different ways to respond. How we choose to think and how we choose to respond are always up to us; if our thoughts and responses aren't bringing us good results, we can learn to think and respond differently. We can learn to use certain ways of thinking to put our-selves in such a frame of mind that we don't need to forgive.

For instance, if someone has done us harm, we can choose to look at it as hurtful but as something that is bringing us a gift. We may not see the gift right away, but we have faith that the gift is there. We can be grateful for the actions that those people took because, by choosing to look at those people as part of a positive movement by the universe to bring us gifts, we will look for those gifts and we will find them. And so, in gratitude for that, we are able to say that, although those people may have had their own motivations and intentions which seemed to be contrary to our greater good, ultimately, they were helping us, and so there is no need to forgive them, because no harm was taken, and in fact only good came our way.

This approach to thinking about what happens to us can help in any situation, not just in hurtful situations. It can make our experi-ences more pleasant, and can improve our relationships with others in many ways.

Our Thinking Affects Everything

As I mentioned earlier, every day, every minute, how we think and how we feel about ourselves affects everything—how we respond to situations, how we feel about ourselves, and all of our relationships (family, friends, lovers, co-workers) in the following ways:

- Whether we like or dislike ourselves, that affects how others treat us.
- Whether we like or dislike others, that affects how we interpret their actions and how we treat others.

If we dislike ourselves or think negatively about ourselves, or if we are habitually suspicious or angry, that affects what we say and how we do things. Our habitual way of thinking comes out in our tone of voice, our body language and how we carry ourselves, and in our choice of words and how we look at the world.

For example, I once commented neutrally to a woman that she was very angry. I could hear it in her voice and see it in how she held her body. She responded with surprise, saying that she was a lot of things, but she wasn't angry. She called me a few weeks later and said that she had been thinking about it and she realized I was right—that she was not only angry, but she was very angry, and angry about a lot of things. She just hadn't been aware of it until I had commented on it.

A low opinion of ourselves is likely to be reflected by others having a low opinion of us as well (unless we are lucky enough to have a very loving person in our lives who chooses to see the best in us rather than the worst that we see in ourselves). If we habitually put ourselves down, what can we expect but that others will agree with us? Some of us play the "feel sorry for me" card, expecting and hoping that others will argue with us and say that we are wrong about ourselves, and sometimes that works. But most people will assume that we know ourselves best, and if we talk down about ourselves, that there must be a reason for it. We are surprised and disappointed when people agree with us. Some of us never catch on to the fact that it was we ourselves who put that thought of our inferiority out there in the first place.

If, on the other hand, we think well of ourselves, are comfortable with who we are, and think well of ourselves, that will also come out in our tone of voice, body language, and choice of words. Even if that confidence and positive self-esteem aren't as warranted as we think they are, that confidence in ourselves encourages others to feel confidence toward us.

Likewise, just as how we think about ourselves affects how others think about us, how we think about others affects our relationships with our family, friends, and coworkers. Whether we are aware of it or not, our habitual manner of thinking comes out in everything we do—in what we say and how we say it, in our body language, in our choice of responses to what other people are saying and doing.

If we are habitually angry or suspicious, even if we try to hide it, or think we are hiding it, people will know. If we are distrustful, and always thinking the worst of people, or we tend to mentally accuse people of crimes we think they committed, those thoughts and that attitude will come through in our words, tone of voice, and facial expressions, and people will respond accordingly. As a result, they might not trust us enough to share important information with us, or they might not trust us enough to share information about themselves because they fear we will use it against them. They certainly won't be open and forthcoming with us. They may also respond negatively, or even leave us.

Our habitual ways of thinking also affect how we interpret the actions of others. If we characteristically assume the worst in people, if we assume that people typically do things deliberately to "get" us or to harm us, then that affects how we think about whatever they are doing. For example, if someone makes a remark that could be taken negatively, positively, or neutrally, some of us will always interpret the remark negatively. Others will typically interpret it positively or neutrally. How we think about the remark doesn't change what the speaker meant; it only changes how we respond to it.

Being Positive Has Positive Results

If we have a clean heart and a positive outlook, people will respond with openness, trust, and warmth. Even if others are habitually suspicious, we can still elicit better responses from them by being positive. (I give a real-life example of this in just a few pages.)

It is also more pleasant and relaxing to be around someone who is positive about themselves; it is tiring to be around someone who is always negative and complaining. As Jo Coudert says in Seven Cats and the Art of Living, "never underestimate the power of cheerfulness." Just as a negative outlook increases stress and places a strain on your body, it also puts a strain on those around you. A positive outlook not only can improve our health and how you feel, it can also attract more positive people to you. A positive outlook improves every situation, and can make a happier and healthier home, family, group of friends, and workplace.

Is It Cool To Be Positive?

Because in some circles it is considered unrealistic to be optimistic or positive, or uncool to feel good about yourself, although some people don't think negatively about themselves or life, they present a jaded or cynical or otherwise negative face to the world. If you are optimistic, some people think you just don't understand what's going on, or that you are being unrealistic. It is almost impossible for some negatively inclined people to imagine people being any other way, and such people will say you are idealistic or unrealistic to think better of humanity than they do.

But it isn't any more realistic to think that the world is going to hell in a hand basket, or that everyone is selfish and only out for themselves, than it is to think that the world is entirely without problems. It is realistic to believe that extremes are less likely to be true than a middle way. Yes, there are bad things happening in the world, but you can choose to change what you pay attention to. You can choose to notice the many good things that are also happening. And yes, there are some people who are selfish, but not everyone is, nor even most people. You can choose to notice the many small courtesies and kindnesses that occur every minute, every day.

Who We Are Colors Our Experiences

Just as how we think about ourselves affects all our relationships, who we are also colors how we look at people. We each tend to habitually have a positive or negative outlook, based on our experiences and the conclusions we've drawn about others. For example, if we are honest and kindly inclined toward others, we tend to assume that others are like that as well. But if we are dishonest or unforgiving, inclined to get revenge on others for imagined slights, then we are more likely to assume that others are like that.

Here's a parable that perfectly illustrates this principle.

A young couple in the later 1800s was traveling by covered wagon through a new settlement. They saw a woman hoeing her garden, so they drew closer to her fence and hailed her. She stopped her hoeing and straightened up, then asked kindly, "What can I do for you, strangers?"

The husband said, "Our old town is too crowded. Land there is hard to find, and expensive when you can find it, so we're looking for a new place to settle. What are folks like around here?"

The woman looked at them and asked, "What are folks like where you come from?"

"They're deceitful!" the husband said.

"And selfish," the wife added.

"And nobody ever helps anyone else," the husband concluded. "We're looking for a place where things are different."

The woman shook her head sadly and said, "I'm sorry, but you'll find that folks around here are just like that. You might as well keep moving on until you find what you're looking for." And so the husband and wife traveled on.

The next day, the same thing happened again. A young couple drove by the woman's yard and hailed her. She stopped her hoeing and straightened up, then asked kindly, "What can I do for you, strangers?"

The husband said, "Our old town is too crowded. Land there is hard to find, and expensive when you can find it, so we're looking for a new place to settle. What are folks like around here?"

Like before, the woman looked at them and asked, "What are folks like where you come from?"

"They're wonderful folk," the husband said.

His wife added, "Everyone is friendly and helpful; honest and upright. We love them dearly, and it was hard to part with them, but we want some land of our own where we can raise a family."

The woman smiled and said, "Why, you'll find that folks here are just like that. Welcome to our town!"

The moral of that story is that much of what we experience arises out of who we are and how we view life. Both couples experienced the things they did because they expected that sort of behavior from others, and they also behaved that way themselves. If you can learn to change your thinking, even a little, you will find that your experience of people will likewise change.

One Person, Two Wildly Different Experiences

In case you are thinking this is just a pretty story, here's a real-life example of how much of a difference your way of thinking about people can have.

One time, many years ago, I was hired as a technical writer by the director of the software division of a company. Until I was hired, writers had always been hired by the manager of the Publications group; it was unprecedented for someone to be hired directly into the software division. But because I was young, I didn't know how things worked. I also didn't know at first that the Publications manager was angry at being bypassed in that manner.

This was back when personal computers were not a normal part of everyday business. This company used mainframes for their programming, and a typing pool for typing up everything. When writing the software manuals, I wrote longhand in pencil on a pad of yellow paper. When I needed my writing typed up, I used the typing pool. The first time I approached the Publications manager for a typist, he assigned me a woman in the pool, telling me that I could use her services as often as I liked; in fact, better yet, I could consider her entirely at my disposal. Everyone else would use the other typists, he said. I thought this was very generous of him.

When I introduced myself to the woman and asked for her help, I could tell that she was a bit angry and suspicious, but I didn't take it personally. And as we spoke, we found we shared several things in common—we both liked the same science fiction authors, and we both enjoyed doing needlework (I sewed and embroidered, she tatted). By the time I walked away, we had the start of a friendship. Over the next several months, as she typed up my work, that friendship continued to grow, and she started to put small, friendly, amusing handwritten notes on the typed pages when she returned them to me.

She always did stellar work for me and got the typed pages back to me on time or early. I was happy with the working relationship and the friendship we had developed.

After I had worked at that company for about six months, the Publications manager thawed toward me in the face of my unrelenting good nature. One day, he invited me to join him for one of the regular lunches that his department had.

During that lunch, he asked me casually how things were working out with the typist. To my puzzlement, a few of the other writers at the table snickered. I replied that I couldn't be happier; that her work was great; that it was beyond criticism and she always got it to me on time. He stared at me and asked if we were talking about the same woman. He then explained that everyone there hated working with her—they found her recalcitrant, uncooperative, always slow in delivering her work to them; there would often be errors in her work, so the writer would have to mark up her work and send it back to her to be redone; and sometimes she would even just flat refuse to do an assignment. In short, he said, he had assigned her to me because he was angry at me for being hired the way I had been. He thought it would be killing two birds with one stone to assign her to me: one, he would get back at me for how I had been hired (though it wasn't my fault that I had been hired that way), and two, he would move a problem person away from his writers. To hear that I was having no problems with her at all astounded him.

I realized then how profoundly effective it is to approach someone with an open mind and to think about them positively. It is possible that had the Publications manager "warned" me about her, prejudicing me against her, I might not have had such a great experience with her, and I would have missed out on a good friendship, not to mention a good work relationship. But he hadn't, and I hadn't, because my outlook was habitually open, optimistic, positive, and friendly, and because I find it easy to genuinely like all kinds of people.

This experience was also a good introduction for me to the idea that our beliefs about reality are not reality itself.

Our Beliefs About Reality Are Not Reality Itself

What do I mean when I say that? I mean that most of what we think is reality is in fact just a belief about reality. In the case of the woman in the typing pool, the people in the Publications department believed that she was a stubborn, uncooperative person who made a lot of mistakes, and that was the woman they experienced. In my experience, she was the opposite. So what was the truth about her? The people in the Publications department never questioned their beliefs about her; they just thought they were right about that woman, and that was as far as they got. They never saw anything to change their opinion about her. And yet, my experience of her was dramatically different from theirs.

One way to think about our beliefs about reality is to consider those beliefs as a map that we are creating while traveling an ever-changing landscape that other people are also traveling. Everyone who travels that landscape creates a map of what it looks like to them, but because the conditions are always changing, and because each person will notice some things and miss other things, no one's map is complete, and there are a lot of differences in our maps. In this analogy, reality is what we travel through; our beliefs are our maps of that reality.

Now let's say we try to share our map (our beliefs) with someone else. Even if we believe our map is accurate, it is still not complete, and the parts we missed or didn't experience won't, of course, be represented on our map.

Our beliefs about reality are very much like that map. They reflect some aspects of reality, but they are not reality itself. Looking at it that way, it can be easier to allow ourselves to accept new information, thereby changing our beliefs about reality.

Using the example of the woman in the typing pool, I had created a map of that woman that was radically different from the map the other people who worked with her had created. When we finally compared notes, it was as though we had traveled in completely different territory, and yet we had all interacted with the same person. I'd like to think that in hearing my experience, they started to change their minds about her, but the point is that what they believed about her couldn't have been the entire truth about her, because I had had such a different experience.

And likewise, what I believed about her wasn't the entire truth of her being, but my approach had brought out a more positive side to her. So even if I wasn't aware of ways in which she could be negative, I was better off knowing her as I did. Even when I found out how others thought about her, it did't change what I believed about her or how I treated her. I preferred my map.

How can thinking of our beliefs this way (i.e., as a map) be helpful? If our map of reality is that life is a shadowy, dangerous place filled with hazards and people who can't be trusted, we'll believe that we have to always be on the lookout. If we realize we created this map while traveling at some midnight of our soul, and that reality can look very different when traveling in the sunny safety of an optimistic day, then we can change our thinking so that we are more relaxed, more open, and more willing to give others the benefit of the doubt instead of suspecting that they mean us harm.

Even if we aren't strongly negative about life, however much we change we attitude toward the positive, we are that much better off, and so will others around us be.

How Can We Change Our Thinking?

So what changes can you make in your life to bring about the ability to see things more positively and experience the better side of more people, as I did with the woman in the typing pool? You might be thinking that was an extraordinary situation or that you don't have it in you to be like that. That is far from the truth. You can do this too.

The first thing to decide is that change is possible. As I mentioned in an earlier chapter, one of the truths of life is that as soon as you decide a solution isn't possible, then it isn't. You won't see the solution, let alone look for it, if you don't think it is there. Likewise, if you don't think change is possible, then it won't be possible for you.

"But wait," you may be saying, "The way I think is the way I think, and there's no changing it." But that is just an idea you have about the way you think about yourself; it isn't the truth about yourself. We all develop ways of thinking about things--positively or negatively, objectively or irrationally, in a biased fashion or neutrally. Some of that arises out of who we are. But who we are arises out of, to a certain extent, how we think and what we think. Perhaps more importantly, who we are also arises out of the decisions we've made about each thing that has happened to us—decisions we've made on how to think about those things, and decisions we've made on how to respond to those things.

Everything that happens can be looked at and interpreted in more than one way. There's a core truth about an event, but then there's also how we think about it. So, for instance, someone we know may do something with a clean heart and positive intentions, but we might decide to be suspicious, paranoid, unfriendly, angry, or unhappy about it. That doesn't change what they did, but it changes how we feel about it and how we respond to it.

And of course, the opposite is true. Someone may say or do something with ill intentions, yet we can choose to interpret that action positively, to think that no harm was meant. Again, that doesn't change what happened itself, but it changes how we think about it, how we feel about it, and how we continue to think about it.

The good news is that, however difficult it can be at first, we can change how we think. If we have a preferred way of thinking about things, and that way is making us unhappy and we'd like to think differently, we can change our thinking. It can take some time and effort to develop a different habit of looking at things positively when we're used to looking at things negatively, but it is possible.

I am not going to say that people are always filled with good intentions, or that you should always think that everyone is trying to do the best they can. That would be flying in the face of our experiences. Lots of people have various sorts of agendas that they are working on, whether at work or in their personal lives, with family and friends. Most of the time people are trying to do the best they can with themselves and others. But sometimes people do mean harm. They truly mean to hurt you or others, or they are devious, or they have ulterior motives or an agenda that includes harming you or others. Sometimes you are on someone's list.

But you have no control over those people. What you do have control over is yourself and how you choose to think about them and what they are doing. What you choose to think affects how you feel about it. This doesn't mean that you are paranoid or a bad person for seeing that someone else is less than perfect. Nor does acknowledging that some people have an agenda, and recognizing what the agenda is, mean that you have to be angry at them for it. It simply means that when you see what they're doing, it is an extra piece of information about them to use when interpreting what they are doing.

The thing to do is to be willing to do whatever it takes to change yourself and your thinking so that you live a life in which the majority of your experiences are positive. Humans being as they are, I can't promise they all will be. But even those experiences that are unpleasant won't leave a lasting mark on you.

It will take some work to change your way of thinking. In the animal kingdom, most animals are beyond forgiving—they don't take offense in the first place. But we humans are different in that we can and do take offense. Sometimes we take offense when offense was meant, and other times we take offense when no offense was meant. In either case, whether harm was meant or not, we take harm, and we blame the other person or persons. Sometimes we are able to let go of it and stop blaming others, and other times we are not.

Nine Principles of the Forgiveness Lifestyle

To change our lives, we need to cultivate our minds; we need to develop or further develop different habits of thinking based on certain principles. In the next set of pages, you'll find descriptions of nine principles that will help you change the times when you are not able to let go to times when you are able to let go. These principles are

1. Honesty
2. Responsibility
3. Generosity of heart
4. Understanding
5. Gratitude
6. Optimism
7. Trust
8. Responding in the moment
9. Finding a gift in every situation

All these principles will help make you change your actions and thoughts so that your experiences are more positive. These principles also come into play when you are using the methods in Chapter 8 to forgive someone. You may already be using some of these habits, but there is deep wisdom on the following pages, so I encourage you to read each section, even if you think you have that habit mastered.

Let's take a closer look at that list of principles and find out what you can do to start making changes in your thinking and therefore in your life. As you read, if you find you disagree with something, that's perfectly okay. You can come up with your own principles if you don't like these. (Though remember what Aristotle said: "It is the mark of an educated mind to be able to entertain a thought without accepting it.")

Also, you don't have to incorporate all these principles into your life at once. That would be too much to ask of yourself. Choose a few principles you think are doable and start putting them into practice. Be okay with not always practicing these new principles. It takes time to change habits. Give yourself that time. You will get there, and each change for the better is a positive thing you have done for yourself. Take time now and then to look back at where you were and compare it with where you are now, and be glad for the changes you have made.

Principle Number 1: Honesty

As a prerequisite to knowledge, understanding, and communication, honesty is essential to changing how you think. If you never hear the truth from yourself and others, you only know an illusion; you only know what someone else wants you to believe about the world or yourself. Yet everyone knows, consciously or unconsciously, when they are being lied to, so they get confused, torn between substance and appearance. The substance is that there is a lie; the appearance is that there is not.

Beyond that confusion, there is a more serious consequence. Lies muddy the waters of any relationship, whether it is family, friends, co-workers, or significant others. Lies make it difficult to know who or what to trust. If someone lies to you and you don't spot the lie, you will respond as though the lie were true, leading to further disrespect on the part of the person doing the lying, and further confusion on your part as that person behaves in ways contrary to what they say. Conversely, if you lie to someone and you believe they haven't caught on, you will become even more disrespectful toward that person. (Although most people know when you are lying and aren't letting you know they know for reasons of their own.)

So why do people lie? Lies arise out of fear. People lie to their loved ones because they are afraid they won't be loved if they tell the truth, or they don't want to have to deal with something they've done. Managers lie to their employees because they are afraid they'll lose respect or they are afraid their employees can't handle the truth or they are afraid of being found out. Employees lie to their managers because they are afraid of losing their job. Parents lie to their children because they are afraid their children can't handle the truth. Children lie to their parents because they fear punishment or withdrawal of love. Arising out of fear as they do, lies likewise spread fear.

None of us likes feeling fearful. On top of the fear that prompted us to lie in the first place, there is always the fear that the lie will be revealed. To be more honest, you'll need to be less afraid. Honesty arises out of trust in oneself and in others, and it also builds trust.

The truth, when kindly told, spreads love.

So the first principle to embrace is to be honest with yourself and others, which means acknowledging the fears that underly any dishonesty you have been practicing.

Honesty and Denial

Honesty means, before anything else, being honest with yourself. It's hard, if not impossible, to be honest with others when you aren't telling yourself the truth.

Being honest with yourself means keeping yourself in the loop on what you are doing and saying. Lying to yourself is a form of denial. In the short term, denial can be a useful way of dealing with something you just aren't ready to face; for example, it can give a buffer time for coming to terms with something drastic that you are experiencing. But denial isn't good if it continues for a long time. In that case, whatever a person is in denial about just never gets dealt with.

Whether we are denying a personal flaw that is interfering with our relationships, or whether we are denying something that has happened externally, denial can lead to a sort of insanity. Each time we lie to ourselves about what is going on inside us or around us, we are denying reality. Each time we deny reality, we cut ourselves off from another piece of reality. If we do that enough, we end up in a tiny world where nothing we think we are experiencing bears any resemblance to what is actually going on.

It took me a long time to see this truth. I've known people who lied to themselves and others about the harmful things they were doing and the effects their actions were having on others. I've also known people who seemed to be conscious and aware most of the time, but were doing or saying things that were not in congruence with other things they were doing or saying.

I used to try to have rational conversations with such people about their actions, only to find that they weren't able to admit, even to themselves, what they had done. Because they had to deny a great deal of what was going on around them to stay in that state of unknowing, their comments on what were real were weird, to say the least, and showed that some very strange movie about what was going on was playing in their heads.

The insidious thing about denial is that, very often, people are in denial about being in denial. They are unaware that they are lying to themselves, and they are unaware that they are lying to themselves about lying to themselves. Like other lies, denial arises out of fear: fear of finding out something about yourself that you are afraid you can't face, fear of facing consequences, or fear of rejection from others.

Such dishonesty profoundly affects our lives.

Putting It Into Practice

Whether you suspect you are in denial or not, the first step toward clarity is to decide to be honest, starting with yourself. If you aren't honest with yourself, then you have lost who you are. If you are honest with yourself but not others, then you have lost a way to connect with people on a profoundly more real level.

When you decide to be honest, you are saying that from this point forward, you want to experience reality as it is, so you are more in sync with those around you. You also open yourself to peace and clarity.

When you make this decision, which is a commitment to yourself, you'll find that the way opens before you to travel further down that path of honesty and self-awareness.

Principle Number 2: Responsibility

Responsibility means accepting that we are in charge of and have control over ourselves and our actions. Not accepting this results in blaming others for our situation.

When we blame others, we are in the mindset of resentment and victimhood. As long as we are in that mindset, it is going to be hard for us to recognize how to get out, because the way we get out is to accept responsibility, which means accepting that we are the one in control of ourselves and your thoughts, not someone else. As described in an earlier chapter, blame and resentment also cause health-challenging changes in our bodies.

Even if someone in our lives does his or her best to control us physically, mentally, or emotionally, nonetheless, we are still the one thinking our thoughts, feeling our emotions, and making our decisions. No one else can cause us to think, feel, or do something different from what we want to do. It's up to us. And when we recognize that truth, then we can see that how or what we think or feel about anything is only up to us, not anyone else.

Note: When we start seeing this truth, if we have been in a deeply painful situation, some very deep issues might be triggered. Don't try to deal with them alone; seek help right away.

Sometimes it's easier to think that someone else is in control. It's easier to blame someone else rather than to recognize that our situation is the result of a series of choices that we have made, especially if we have dug ourselves into a very deep hole. But because we dug that hole, we can dig ourselves out of it; no one else can do that for us.

Sometimes we think (or say) that the other person "made" us do something, including "made" us think or feel this way. But nobody can make us think or feel anything that we don't want to think or feel.

How we think about a situation, whether we blame others in the situation, or whether we accept that they did what they did and we have chosen to respond to it in a particular way, affects how easily that we will be able to let go of and move through the pain, the anguish, the hurt, the anger. As long as we believe that we are a victim, that belief itself, those thoughts bring about certain chemical and emotional changes that cause us to feel even more distressed, more in chaos, less in control.

The Solution to Blame is to Accept Responsibility

The solution to blame is to accept responsibility. Start believing that you are in control of your thoughts, and of your reactions to what others say and do. Choose to see that you are in control. (Because you are in control, whether you want to think that you are or not.)

It can be very difficult to move out of feelings of resentment and blame. So difficult, that it might seem easier to stay there. It takes work, it takes accepting responsibility, it takes noticing what needs to be done, it takes being aware of the right thing to do in a situation. It means changing habits of thought that you may be quite comfortable with, or might not even be aware of. Yet as long as you believe that someone else is in charge, as long as you blame them, then you are not looking at what you can do to make the situation better.

It can be hard to change habits of thought that you have developed over many years or decades, thoughts that say you are not in control, thoughts that are resentful and blaming. But every change you make to those thoughts, every time you decide to think more positively about something, to see yourself as the person in charge of yourself, you become more powerful and more in charge of your own life in a conscious and deliberate way. You stop allowing life to happen to you. You stop reacting to life in an unconscious and random way. You start responding to life in more joyful, conscious, and healthy ways.

"Responsibility" can be a scary word to some people, but it can be very liberating to accept responsibility for your life. When you realize that you are in charge of your feelings, and that sometimes you have been your own worst enemy because of how you've been thinking about someone or something, then you also realize how much you want to change that thing about yourself. You can also realize that you can change how you feel by changing how you think about things and people.

As you choose to think more optimistic thoughts, more responsible thoughts, more philosophical thoughts, then that creates healthy chemical changes in your brain and body, so that you feel better, you feel calmer, you feel more centered, you are more able to look rationally at a situation, and you feel better about yourself.

Putting It Into Practice

To start becoming more responsible, try saying to yourself that you are in control, and that nobody is to blame for your life. What happens when you say that to yourself? What thoughts and feelings come up? Do you feel anger? Do you feel fear? Just notice for now; don't get too involved in trying to explain your reactions or argue against the idea. When something happens that you are inclined to blame others for, ask yourself if there is a way in which you can accept responsibility for your reaction to a situation.

Or is blame even appropriate in a situation? For example, could the situation be viewed more neutrally, without assigning blame or fault to anyone? Sometimes things just happen and that's the way they are; there's no need to assign blame. Instead, you can just shrug and move on. For example, I once had to visit a body shop to consult about my car. I called right before going over there and was told they would be open until five o'clock. When I arrived, they had closed at four and the consultation wasn't possible. Rather than blaming them, I had a pleasant chat with the one remaining employee, and rescheduled an appointment for the next day. Then, so the trip wasn't wasted, I went to Trader Joe's, which was nearby, to pick up some staples we were out of.

You can also ask yourself if there is a way in which you can release judgments or preconceptions or prejudices about even a small aspect of what happened, without judging yourself or invalidating your feelings.

Then, if it feels comfortable to you, choose one thing you have been blaming someone else for that you know (or suspect) in your heart you are responsible for, and acknowledge your responsibility for that thing. Choose something small and unimportant. Pay attention to how that feels. Do you feel a sense of relief and freedom, as though a weight has been lifted from you? Or do you feel angry and even more resentful? Are you arguing with me right now, telling me how wrong I am and asking me how could I possibly say that you are responsible for that thing? Pay attention to your arguments. As Richard Bach said in his book Illusions, "Argue for your limitations and they are yours." Why are you arguing that you are not responsible for your own life and your own thoughts, or not in control of your own life? Are our afraid of being responsible for and in charge of your own life? Are you afraid you will have to clean up your own messes? Are you afraid of how others will respond to you accepting responsibility for your own life?

One book that can help with this process of learning to see how we are each responsible for our own thoughts is Ingrid Katal's book, *What Is Your Honor Code?* Ingrid's book is a treasure house of ways to assess yourself and your life to find greater happiness.

Principle Number 3: Generosity of Heart

A certain generosity of heart is important for living forgivingly. It can be a good habit to get into to find something good and praiseworthy in every person you meet, especially those whom you are inclined to judge as unworthy or lacking in some way. When you do this, it can help make whatever situation you are in with that person be less onerous. Also when you do this, that person will respond, even if you never say anything to them. They will pick up on your positive thoughts through your body language or some other way, and can't help but respond, even if a tiny bit.

Putting It Into Practice

When you're considering the actions of another, be willing to make allowances. Giving them a little leeway helps speed the process of forgiving people both for past transgressions and in the moment. It also helps develop a state of mind and a way of thinking about and responding to situations, so that you don't need to forgive in the first place, because you aren't feeling unforgiving toward that person. Along the way, you can also develop a greater understanding of others, which in turn leads to compassion.

If you want to get annoyed or be frustrated about something, go ahead and do it, but don't lash out at others. It's important to acknowledge to yourself what you are feeling. One reason why we hold grudges is because sometimes we just didn't let ourselves fully feel our feelings at the time something happened; we instead held back from expressing ourselves, or letting ourselves know just how profoundly we were affected.

Principle Number 4: Understanding

Understanding is a key element of living forgivingly. Part of any process of living forgivingly is coming to a greater understanding of the situation and the people involved, and accepting that people are who they are. This doesn't mean you condone what happened; it just means that you better understand things. This principle also applies to living forgivingly. In my experience, the better we understand anything—a person, situation, event, or thing, whatever it might be, whether it is hurtful, frustrating, or angering, the better we feel about that person or thing. And it also to a certain extent can mean that, once you have come to an understanding of what happened, you find that what happened wasn't a bad thing. I'm not talking about things that were truly harmful; I am talking about things that you took harm from that perhaps you didn't need to. Sometimes we take offense when no offense was meant. Sometimes we decide we have been injured when in fact no such thing happened.

The United States Constitution declares that all men are created equal. But as a friend once pointed out, that doesn't mean we are all the same. Some of us are smarter, some are wiser, some are kinder, some are more perceptive, some are more athletic. Each of us has a unique combination of gifts, talents, and challenges. We all have equal rights, and we are all equally valuable as human beings, but we are not all equal.

Whatever you are, not everyone is. You may be thoughtful; not everyone is. You may be efficient and productive; again, not everyone is. Rejoice in what you are, but don't expect everyone to be like you, and don't judge them as less worthy, and certainly don't hold who they are against them.

Conversely, if you tend to be impatient and make snap judgments, or if you tend to be unrelenting, vengeful, and unforgiving, don't assume that everyone is like you, and don't respond to them as though they are. You'll cheat yourself out of a lot of good relationships that way.

Bear this in mind when considering what others have done, especially when considering something someone has done that we find unfathomable. Because it is human nature to judge others by what we are like, if we are kind, we expect others to be kind. If we know we are not trustworthy, then we expect others to be untrustworthy. The more we understand ourselves, the easier it can be to understand others.

As Louise Hay once said, "We cannot force others to change. We can offer them a positive mental atmosphere where they have the possibility to change if they wish. But we cannot do it for, or to, other people. Everyone is here to work out their own lessons, and it we fix it for them, then they will just go and do it again, because they have not worked out what they needed to do for themselves. All we can do is love them. Allow them to be who they are. Know that the truth is always within them and that they can change at any moment they want." (Though it can help to speak up and maybe plant a seed or two.)

The Sun Rises Every Day, But Most People Don't Wake Up

Part of understanding is not making assumptions about the state other people are in. My natural tendencies are to be idealistic. Because of this, I used to assume everyone is alert, aware, and paying attention, and that therefore, whatever they are doing, they must be doing on purpose. Not believing that many people simply weren't paying attention, I often grew annoyed when people did thoughtless, oblivious things.

Then Dan Duggan, a teacher at Santa Clara University, told me that most people walk around asleep. He explained what he meant by that: that most people are unaware and unconscious of themselves and their actions, and therefore, whatever they are doing, they are doing in a kind of sleep-walking state. When he said this, I thought it was a rather jaundiced view of humanity, and I didn't want to believe it.

But I soon figured out that Dan's attitude doesn't have to be seen as a jaundiced view of humanity. It can be taken to be a neutral view of people, neither judging people as good or bad, but just saying that's how it is. The sun rises every day, but most people don't wake up. I realized that if I can adjust my thinking to look at it that way, then when someone does something that seems deliberately rude, I can tell myself that it might not, after all, be deliberate; that they might not have meant to cause harm. This way of thinking is acceptable to me because I also believe that everyone is essentially good; people don't usually go around doing things that are rude or inconsiderate and harmful on purpose.

Likewise, if you adjust your thinking about the underlying reasons for people doing what they do in a similar way, you'll reduce your stress about everyday interactions. This approach isn't making excuses for people, but is instead a way of thinking about how and what people do so that you don't end up thinking hard, unhappy thoughts about people.

If you think that thinking this way about other people is unrealistic or is letting them off a hook, think of the times when you have unknowingly been rude or careless; for example, when you are driving, and you unknowingly and unintentionally cut someone off, or you block someone from making a turn because you were hogging the lane, and you don't realize that you were doing so. You don't judge yourself for those lapses. You don't think to yourself that you did it on purpose or that you meant to do harm. Instead, you know in your heart that you didn't mean to do any harm; that you were, essentially, innocent of any wrongdoing. So when you realize you've done something like this, you think to yourself, "Well, it happens, and I didn't mean it." And you forgive yourself easily; you know that it was a mistake. You try not to do it, but it occasionally happens.

Putting It Into Practice

If you apply that kind of thinking to other people when you are inclined to blame them for something they've done, but there is a reasonable doubt about their intentions (that they might not have meant it, which for many people is the case), then you will find that you respond to such actions in a much more relaxed manner. In other words, if you change your thinking about a situation, you'll find it easier to not hold it against that person. That's one less time in your day of feeling anger.

Principle Number 5: Gratitude

What is lack of forgiveness but the absence of thankfulness for what you have? The absence of appreciation for the experience? Another habit you can cultivate is to be grateful. Gratitude will help you keep from hanging onto resentment and anger, just as the habit of making allowances can help you from holding onto those feelings. Gratitude has the power to bring joy to your heart, and there are so many things you can be grateful for. Even if things are grim, there is always something you can find to be thankful for.

It is easier to notice what's being done wrong than to notice what others are doing right. Part of this is because we expect things to go well. We expect them to be done right. It is when they aren't done right that it stands out. For example, when driving, we often experience bad driving by others, but we often also experience courtesy from others—someone who lets us cut in front of them, someone who slows down for us, someone who is paying attention to the road and not texting. But because we expect these courtesies, we don't notice them. Teach yourself to notice, then give thanks for those times when someone is courteous. When people do something right, say "thank you" (whether out loud or mentally, it doesn't matter). Say it nicely, not dismissively, with genuine gratitude for their courtesy. For example, when someone lets you merge into a lane, say "thank you."

Look around to find what else you can find that you can appreciate. Is there something about what you are experiencing right now that you can view with gratitude?

There are so many areas in which you can be thankful; for instance, broad categories of people, nature, natural structures, human made structures, our planetary system, the sun, or universe. You can be grateful for systems within nature; for instance, animal companions—cats, dogs, fish, birds; wild animals—deer, foxes, bear, elk, moose. You can be grateful for rivers, streams, waterfalls, lakes, the ocean; mountains, trees, wildflowers, a cool breeze, a warm breeze, electrical storms, gentle rains.

You can be grateful for the people in your life—family, friends, people who support you, strangers who smile at you; the gift of conversation, companionship; foods; different cuisines—international, local, culinary delights of all sorts, from hush puppies to the fancy stuff. Opportunities that you've had that you've taken advantage of. Even opportunities that you didn't take advantage of. These are all things that you can be thankful for. It can be overwhelming to think of how much you have to be thankful for. So focus on just one thing each day if you'd like, and give thanks for it.

Even thinking of one good thing will lighten your heart. It can bring a smile to your face and can clear out a lot of the darker feelings that negative thoughts can elicit. If the only thing you can say is, "Well, the sun is shining," or "There are lovely trees on the road," or "I have a wonderful, loving, purring cat on my lap" (assuming you like cats and you have a cat), then that's great! Just think about anything, even something that might seem little or insignificant to you, that you appreciate and that you are grateful for.

Gratitude won't make whatever you are experiencing go away (though it might), but it will help you feel better in the moment. And it will also help you when such things happen again. Once you find one thing to appreciate, you'll find it's easier to find another, and then another, and another...until it becomes a habit to focus on what is good and what you can be grateful for.

Putting It Into Practice

If you choose to find something to be grateful for in a situation, you are less likely to hold onto that situation for a long time, or to take harm from it in such a way that you will have to later forgive the people involved.

Principle Number 6: Optimism and a Positive Outlook

Optimism is related to gratitude, and having a positive attitude is related to both gratitude and optimism. All three approaches focus on what is good

- With gratitude, the focus is on what you have already received and on what is good and right in your life rather than on what is bad and wrong. Gratitude has already been discussed in the previous section.
- With optimism, the focus is on what you expect to experience.
- With a positive outlook, the focus is on finding a positive way of thinking about what is happening or what has happened.

Optimism is a habit of thinking; it is the belief that a positive outcome is possible. How many times have you heard someone say, when something bad happens to them, "Just my luck"? When they say that, they are expressing their expectation that a negative outcome is normal for them. An optimistic way of thinking about that something bad that happened is to assure yourself that such things happen but they don't have to be the norm for you.

Optimism itself, coupled with a positive outlook, can bring about a more positive outcome; often, when we expect the best from others or a situation, we receive it, as described earlier in the example of the woman in the typing pool. And also, when we express to ourselves and others the expectation that everything will turn out fine, we help build that expectation, so that our optimism becomes a self-fulfilling prophecy.

I'm not recommending a perky denial of what's going on in your life. If something sad is happening, then sadness is appropriate. What I am recommending is making optimism your habitual way of thinking. In developing a more optimistic attitude, you develop mental pathways of peace and acceptance, rather than turmoil and rejection or blame. Optimism is a choice, a choice you can choose to make any time.

Forgiveness, Love, and Fear

Optimism is a way in which we can choose love. According to *A Course in Miracles*, whenever we make a decision, take an action, or say something, we are increasing fear or extending love. Fear leads to contraction, failure, and death. Love leads to expansion, success, and life. Whenever you make a choice based in fear, you are choosing to go in the direction of death. Likewise, when you make a choice based in love, you are making a choice for life.

Many people aren't consciously aware of this principle, and of those who are aware, many are not aware that this principle applies not just to individuals, it also applies to any kind of group—family, circle of friends, a company, a city, a nation. Whenever you get more than one person involved, you have a group consensus (not necessarily consciously), so that that group of people is normally choosing one of those two modalities—fear or love.

When you visit someone's home, you can sometimes tell what the predominant choice (fear or love) is. In some people's homes, you feel welcome, you feel safe; if you are staying as a guest, you might get some of the best rest you've ever had.

On the other hand, at some people's homes, you feel uncomfortable or unwelcome, even though the people may seem friendly or even gracious. And if you sleep there, you might have nightmares. You don't like being there.

These examples are at the family level. Whoever lives in those homes has chosen one or the other way—fear or love.

The same goes for a company (a workplace). As part of creating the (often unstated and even unconscious) corporate culture, the people within a company participate in making decisions that promote either fear or love. In a loving workplace, you might have a few individuals who predominantly make decisions and take actions based in fear; likewise, in a fear-based corporate climate, you might have a few individuals who make decisions and take actions based in love. In either case, the person whose choices are the opposite of the company's preferred choices overall will eventually leave, because they don't fit in with the company's unspoken culture.

Ultimately, fear-based families and companies will not thrive; contrariwise, people who choose to extend love will thrive no matter what others around them try to do.

Putting It Into Practice

Here's a wonderful thing about this: these are all choices that individuals are making. Because they are all choices, each member of a family or company can make a different choice. If you have chosen to extend fear, you can choose to extend love from now on. It doesn't matter how many times you've chosen fear; you can choose love the next time. Being optimistic is one way to do so.

Principle Number 7: Trust

Related to optimism is trust. To recap the previous section, optimism is the belief that a positive outcome is possible. In a general sense, trust is the expectation that there will be positive outcome, even if things seems grim. On the more personal level, in terms of trusting the people in your life, trust means you believe that they want good things to happen to you, and therefore won't deliberately harm you, nor will they allow others to do harmful things to you if they can help it. You trust that they will be honest with you, and will do what they can to be loving and compassionate toward you. In this book, the focus is on the first, more general sense, not in the more personal sense.

It is difficult to be in the middle of a bad situation and find any sense of trust that it will all come out okay. But becoming stressed about what is happening, and focusing on what you fear will be the outcome, can prevent you from seeing what you can do to make things better. If you can relax enough to tell yourself that everything will be okay no matter what the appearances, then you will immediately improve the situation, if only in how you are feeling about and dealing with it.

Paradoxically, sometimes telling yourself that the worst is going to happen can help you calm down so you can handle the situation more rationally. In 2013, former Army Staff Sergeant Clint L. Romesha received the Medal of Honor from President Obama for fighting off an attack in Afghanistan in 2009. As Obama said, "What happened ... has been described as one of the most intense battles of the entire war in Afghanistan. The attackers had the advantage, the high ground, the mountains above, and they were unleashing everything they had -- rocket-propelled grenades, heavy machine guns, mortars, snipers taking aim." And yet, despite the overwhelming odds, Romesha and his team, through acts of great courage, managed to save lives and re-trieeve the bodies of their dead companions. In an interview, Romesha explained that he decided early on in the fight that he wasn't going to get out of the attack alive, so he was able to think clearly and calmly.

It can be helpful to think about past situations and notice what good came out of them. If you are tempted to think that nothing good came of them, think again. I'll say more about this in the next section on finding the gift in every situation. For now, the reason for noticing what good came out of a past bad situation is to give yourself more reasons for trusting that good can come out of a current situation.

Use Your Imagination to Build Trust

Your imagination is one of the most powerful tools you have at your disposal. Among other applications of your imagination, you can use it to expand your sense of trust.

Try this experiment: imagine that everyone you think is trying to harm you is actually trying to help you in some way. You may not be able to immediately see how, but tell yourself to take it on faith that they are. Even if you balk at the idea of thinking something like this, notice how, with that thought, some part of you relaxed a little, felt a little less afraid or injured or helpless about your situation. Even if you told yourself this was just your imagination, you still responded. The mind and body are powerfully connected; decades of research into the mind-body connection have shown this. What we think affects our emotions. Our emotions affect our bodies.

Now take it a step further: as you imagine that everyone is trying to help you, start imagining ways in which this could be true. Perhaps you are in the wrong place or job or relationship, and perhaps there is something better for you if only you have the courage to move away from where you are now. Now imagine that the people you think are harming you also know this on some level, and are doing what they can, in the only way they know how, to help you move. Now imagine that you can see how it is that what those people are doing is helpful. (This is one way to find the gift in a situation, about which, more later.)

This isn't to say that you should allow people to mistreat you, because you shouldn't. But this book isn't about handling abusiveness or abusive relationships (though it is about learning how to forgive that kind of treatment). There are many fine resources (friends, counselors, books, Web sites) that can help you learn to recognize abuse and learn to respond appropriately, and to take care of yourself and keep yourself safe.

Putting It Into Practice

Experiment with looking at your experiences from a different perspective. You can find that changing how you look at things will also change how you react to them and how you feel about them. It can help you develop a greater sense of trust for yourself and others. It can help you be calmer and less stressed about a current situation, and it can help you release some old emotions about situations in your past.

Principle Number 8: Responding In The Moment

When something happens, we can make it better by responding to it in the moment. If we are angry, let ourselves be angry. Likewise if we are hurt, sad, or feeling any other emotion. When we do this,

- We can take care of ourselves and our responses right then and there, instead of going into denial or hiding away from ourselves or not sharing what's going on with us with others who are involved.

- We can also view the situation or person with forgiving eyes, not holding against them whatever they might have done before. It is possible to experience a person differently, sometimes in an entirely different way, by not holding things against them.

By responding in the moment, we won't hold onto feelings and thoughts arising out of that experience. If we are angry, and allow ourselves to be angry, then in expressing that anger in the moment, we don't keep it stuffed and hidden.

Changing How We Think

We are always interpreting what other people are saying and doing. I use the word "interpreting" because seldom can we know what is truly going on with them. So it boils down to this: things happen, people say things, people do things, events occur, and we interpret all of that according to our beliefs, thought habits, and filters. We tell ourselves what to think about it, and then we think that.

So we can affect our experiences by developing a habit of interpreting events positively, of giving people the benefit of the doubt, of coming up with alternative explanations for someone's actions. This does not mean making excuses for them, but is instead finding more ways in which we can look at something. For example, if someone snaps at us, instead of telling ourselves that they were attacking us personally, we can say to ourselves, "Okay, maybe that person is just having a bad day. Maybe their grumpiness has nothing to do with me. They might have a physical issue that's bothering them and making them not able to be at their best. They might be concerned about something in their life, a concern that is distracting them and keeping them from being focused on the here and now." This is just an example; there are so many things that you can say to yourself to make allowances for the broad range of human experience, and for you not being the target, but instead just being an observer, someone who happens to be involved with something that is going on.

Putting It Into Practice

By developing this habit of thinking, you'll find that you don't hold onto stuff. You won't hold grudges, or maybe you won't hold on to them nearly as long. You might be temporarily annoyed or angry or upset (which is normal and fine), but you won't continue to feel that way; you won't hold onto those feelings, and therefore you won't have yet another little bit of emotional debris that you're hanging onto, an emotional weight that's weighing you down, debris that is accumulating in the clear waters of your emotional experience in this life.

When you have something more serious that you're dealing with, the habit of making allowances and of focusing on what is right in your life can help lighten your load even when a grievance is bothering you. So instead of focusing on that grievance 24/7 for a long time, you can lift your thoughts and lift your heart by asking yourself, "What is good that is going on in my life?"

Principle Number 9: Find The Gift

The final thought habit to develop is to find the gift in every situation. This is a more expanded version of what I just described under "Trust" (finding the good that might have come out of a bad situation). In that case, you were looking for a general good. In this case, you are specifically looking for something good that happened that is a gift to you. The kinds of gifts we can find in any situation include

- Learning something new about someone else or people in general that makes it easier to understand and interact with others, such as learning to understand different types of personalities so you can better communicate with different kinds of people.

- Learning something new about ourselves that makes life easier. For example, we might learn that we prefer one type of situation over another, so that we can keep ourselves out of the types of situations we don't like.

- Moving from a bad situation to a better one (or even a great one), such as moving to a new and better home, getting a new job that is more fulfilling, or leaving a bad relationship and finding a better one.

- Gaining a new friend or family member.

- Changing a habit we didn't like but couldn't change before.

- Finding out that we can survive bad things and continue to not only live, but to thrive.

- Learning a new skill.

- Overcoming a fear.

- Resolving a long-term issue with someone.

Here's an example of how we can find a gift in even the most horrendous of circumstances. In 2010, Marine Lance Corporal William "Kyle" Carpenter (now retired) was severely injured when he threw himself into the path of a grenade to shield a fellow Marine against the blast. His jaw was shattered, he lost an eye, and he suffered other injuries. He spent two and a half years in the hospital undergoing surgery. Although many might think him entitled to be angry or bitter over his injuries, he is not. Instead, he was able to find something good in his experience. According to the Marine Corps, Carpenter said, "I look back and I'm actually very appreciative I had those two and a half years, because those years put things in perspective more than a whole lifetime of things could if I wasn't there." He received the Medal of Honor, the United Sates' highest military honor, on June 19, 2014.

Finding Meaning is a Choice

Although Carpenter found a meaningful gift in his circumstances, sometimes when something happens that brings good, we choose to consider that good result to be chance or a coincidence, rather that something that has meaning. But is a it is a choice, not a fact, to thinking of the gift as a random coincidence. And believing that something was random and not meaningful can cause pain because it can make you feel more cut off from others and from the good that life can bring you.

Just as it is a choice to believe that something is not meaningful, it is a choice to believe that something is meaningful. And so, because it is a choice, why not choose to believe that whatever happened was meaningful? Why not choose to believe that it is in fact helpful or synchronous? And why not choose to look for the gift in the situation? Especially because thinking this way will help you feel better.

Here's another example of finding the gift in a situation. I once rented a house nestled among redwoods near the Northern California coast. The house was cantilevered over a steep slope above a small creek. The house had many flaws, but it had potential and I loved the location. When I first moved in, the owner asked if I was interested in purchasing it. I said I would think about it.

After living there a few months, I wrote to her to tell her I would very much love to purchase the house. The owner wrote back and said that she wasn't interested in selling it and had never been interested in selling it; she didn't know where I had gotten the idea that she was. I was very disappointed by the owner's odd change of heart. However, three months later, while I was at work, a neighbor called to tell me that the house was sliding down the slope. I rushed home to find that "sliding down the slope" was a bit of an exaggeration, but close enough to the truth to be alarming. The foundations of the pillars holding up the cantilevered part had only been set in the topsoil, not into the bedrock. When a large patch of land supporting those pillars slipped, the pillars started to go with the slipping land. The entire northwest corner of the house was slumping down at an alarming angle.

This turn of events was a shock. I was afraid to even go inside the house; the land was still slipping and I didn't know whether the house would continue to support any weight. The county inspectors red-tagged the house (that means "unsafe to live in"), and the propane gas providers removed the propane tank (which sat right above the slip point, so it was in danger of going down the slope).

Temporarily homeless, I hired movers to pack up everything and put it in storage for a few months while I looked for another place to rent. (During that time, I moved in with a friend who generously opened his home to me.) But rentals were expensive and hard to find, so I decided to see if I could qualify to purchase a house. The answer was yes; the housing market was at a low at the time, and I quickly found a lovely, affordable house.

The two obvious gifts arising out of that situation are this:

1. Had I purchased that house in the redwoods, I would have had the expense and inconvenience of dealing with the damage caused by the slippage, which I could not afford.

2. With the difficulty of finding a place to rent, I became open to the possibility of owning my own home, with the result of finding a home I love.

Although I am happy with these gifts, if I wanted to look more, I could find more gifts arising out of that situation.

Putting It Into Practice

You can apply this approach to anything that happens in your life. Look for the positive good that came out of it. It could be that you got a better job, or learned something about human nature, or learned something about your own approach to life; you might have learned a new skill, or overcome a fear, or gained a new friend. All of those are gifts that can arise from what might seem a bad situation.

When you believe that a gift is there, you'll look for it. When you look for it, you'll find it. When you find it, you'll feel better about yourself, the situation, and the other people involved.

It may seem obvious, but when you develop this habit of looking for a gift, you will find more and more gifts in your life, and your attitude toward life will be more positive and optimistic

Everything Can Teach You

A final note before we move on to the next chapter: everything can teach you, but only if you're willing to learn. No matter how rich your environment, no matter how willing and helpful others around you are, if you're not willing to learn from a situation and if you don't apply yourself to learning from it, you won't. This is your prerogative;

that's free will. But if you don't learn from a situation, you will keep repeating the same mistakes.

Chapter 5

Willingness
is Essential

We can't do anything if we aren't willing to do it. This is especially true for forgiveness. Being willing to forgive takes you halfway there to forgiveness.

"Most people don't have that willingness to break bad habits. They have a lot of excuses and they talk like victims."
Carlos Santana

What Is willingness, and why is it important? Willingness is the precursor to reaching any goal. We cannot reach a goal unless we are willing to do what it takes to reach that goal. Likewise, willingness is the horse that draws the cart of forgiveness. In order to forgive, we must be willing to forgive—if only just a bit. We don't have to feel good about that person or the situation. We don't even have to be completely willing to forgive; we only need to be willing to forgive some piece of a situation, or some aspect of something someone did. If we are not willing to forgive, we just won't be able to do it. Even if it is just a tiny amount of willingness, that small willingness is all we need to move forward. As we work through what we are willing to work through, more willingness will come.

It can be tougher to be willing to forgive than it is to forgive. You may think you aren't ready or willing to forgive, and perhaps mostly you are not. Yet even if you are protesting and saying that you don't want to forgive, if there is any part of you that is convinced that forgiveness is a good thing, then to that extent, you are willing to forgive. Whether it is a general willingness to forgive, or a willingness to forgive someone or something specific, that willingness is key. Maybe you aren't willing to forgive everything, but that's okay. Forgiving everything at once is not impossible, but it certainly isn't easy. Nor is it necessary. Just take it one step at a time, and you'll get there.

Willingness Isn't Forgiveness

Willingness itself is not the same as the thing you are willing to do. In the case of forgiveness, willingness to forgive doesn't mean you have already forgiven. If it did, how easy it would be! Instead, you must take the first step toward forgiveness while you are still in an unforgiving state. You will still be feeling such things as anger, anguish, fear, resentment, doubt, and pain, but if you are willing to move through and beyond those feelings so you are no longer holding them inside, you will be able to start forgiving.

Let's take the example of swimming. Let's say you can't swim, but you want to be able to. In this case, you are willing to swim, and the willingness to swim is essential for you to begin swimming, but you can't actually swim yet. Because you are willing to swim, you'll be willing to do whatever it takes to learn how to swim.

In the context of forgiveness, being willing to forgive is not forgiveness itself, but it is necessary for forgiving. You cannot forgive until you are willing to forgive. Once you are willing to forgive, you'll do whatever it takes to forgive.

Willingness is one of the hardest aspects of forgiveness. In some cases, finding that willingness to forgive can take you halfway to forgiveness.

The Island of Forgiveness

Let's take the swimming analogy a bit further. Let's say that forgiveness is like a large and beautiful island in the middle of a lake. The island is lovely and peaceful, populated with all manner of loving birds and animals and people. Delicious fruits and berries, always in season, are ready for the picking, and brilliantly colored flowers bloom, visited by hummingbirds and the gently humming bees. Tall, nurturing trees shade the edges of wide, sunlit meadows. Cool, refreshing waters flow from pure springs. Whoever you meet on this island is a friend, and the animals never sting or bite. In the evenings, you sit with your friends on the veranda of a tall, comfortable house and talk about the day's events. Later, after a wholesome, delicious, home-cooked meal, you go to sleep in the most comfortable bed you have ever had the pleasure of lying in. While on that island, you experience a deep and satisfying sense of peace that radiates from your core and affects how you see everything.

Lovely and desirable as it is, the only way to get to that island is to swim. No one can take you there; there are no boats or flying machines to give you a shortcut. You yourself must decide you want to go. You yourself must wade into the lake's waters. You yourself must move your arms and legs and body with enough skill to get yourself from the shore to the island.

So two things are needed in order to achieve your goal of reaching that island: the ability to swim, and your willingness to get into that water and swim to that island. You can learn the ability; someone can teach you how to swim by showing you how to float and how to move your body and your arms and your legs. However, the willingness is yours and yours alone. Nobody is going to throw you into the lake and force you to swim. You have to decide to go in willingly. Even if you know how to swim, you have to make that first step into the water to put those swimming skills into practice.

And you might have all kinds of reasons for not wanting to go in. The water might be cold, or the waves rough, or you might think you don't have the stamina to make it there. Or perhaps you just don't want to get wet. But that island calls to you, so in you go. It can be hard going at first, but after a while, you find it easier and easier to move through the lake toward your goal.

Your willingness to forgive is that first step into the water. It is a commitment to yourself to do whatever it takes to move through the sometimes rough waters of your thoughts and feelings to get to that island on the lake. That one simple decision sets into motion everything you need to reach your goal.

This book is one way you can learn the techniques of forgiveness—it teaches you how to swim, in effect. It also gives you more information on willingness, so that you can find it easier to decide to be willing. But the decision to be willing to forgive is up to you.

How Do You Become More Willing?

If you weren't before, you may now be willing to be willing, and that's a great start. But, you ask, how can one go about becoming more willing? The short answer is, you just decide to do it.

The longer answer is, your willingness might require a bit of digging into your thoughts about the person or situation. If you ask yourself whether you are willing to forgive someone and your answer is "no," then you'll need to ask yourself some other questions. Why are you unwilling to forgive that person or situation? That question can open the door to a host of reasons. Perhaps you are afraid that if you forgive them, your forgiveness

- invalidates the pain you are feeling
- means nothing bad happened
- makes whatever they did okay
- means you made a mistake in some way

Fortunately, those fears can be addressed.

Forgiveness isn't about saying that the other person is right and you are wrong. Your pain is real. Nor is it about denying that anything happened. It did happen. Nor does forgiveness mean that you have to say that whatever happened was okay, even in the cosmic sense.

Clearly what happened wasn't okay, or you wouldn't be feeling this way. And while it is possible that you did make a mistake, the process of forgiveness I describe in this book can help you come to a greater understanding that puts the event in a positive light, and perhaps might help you see that some positive good came out of the situation.

But although understanding those truths intellectually may come more easily, feeling them emotionally can take a while longer. If you can decide that you are mentally willing to forgive a person or a situation, even while acknowledging that you are still in a black hole of emotional turmoil, then that is all you need. You just need a little willingness; the rest will come.

If you are finding it hard to be willing to forgive one person, but easier to be willing to forgive another, then choose the easier person first. The more people you forgive, the easier it becomes to forgive others.

And it might help to remind yourself that you are doing this for yourself; that you are choosing to forgive so you can be healthier and happier.

Letting People Be Who They Are

An especially difficult reason for not being willing to forgive is when someone isn't doing anything to hurt you on purpose. There might be nothing wrong with what they are doing, but you are upset by what they are doing and how they are doing it. It can be quite a struggle to wrestle with your outrage and disappointment to the point where you are willing to just let them be who they are without thinking they are wrong in being that person.

What If You Aren't Willing to Forgive?

I have successfully used the principles and practices I describe in this book many, many times to forgive someone, something, some situation, some group of people—forgive them to the point where I no longer have any uncomfortable thoughts or feelings about them or the situation.

I have also chosen to not forgive certain people for a while—sometimes even a long while. That was my choice. I just was not willing yet to forgive them. Yet the more I practiced forgiving others, the less sense it made to not forgive those people. However, at first I was unwilling to forgive them, and I let myself be okay with that.

Willingness to forgive can take time. I worked for years on forgiving some people who had done me a great deal of deep and long-term harm. I was gradually able to come to a better place mentally and emotionally about those people, but it took me a long time to fully forgive a few of them because I hadn't been willing to completely let go of everything. Once I was able to be willing to completely forgive those people, I was able to work through the remaining hurt that I had in regard to them. But I allowed myself to not forgive them while I worked on the easier events and the easier people to forgive.

I am saying this because you may find that you aren't willing at the moment to forgive someone (or many someones), and you are judging yourself for that lack of willingness or are trying to force yourself to be willing. It's a lot to ask of yourself to be willing to forgive everyone at once, and it isn't necessary. It's okay if you just are not ready to forgive some people. Just tell yourself that "no only means no for now," meaning that you are allowing the possibility that at some point in the future, that "no" will turn into a "yes."

One fundamental aspect of forgiveness is acceptance, and that applies to you as surely as it applies to those you are choosing to forgive (or not forgive). So accept yourself as you are in the moment. You are traveling toward a new state of awareness and love; don't expect yourself to be at your destination before you have made the trip. Better yet, enjoy the journey!

Chapter 6

Asking for Help is Human

Many of us look at "help" as a dirty word: it is either shameful or embarrassing to ask for, let alone need, help. But we are all alive because of help, and life itself is a vast matrix of people helping people, whether we see it or not. Understanding this, we can more easily ask for and receive help when we are working on forgiving someone.

"None of us got to where we are alone. Whether the assistance we received was obvious or subtle, acknowledging someone's help is a big part of understanding the importance of saying thank you."
Harvey Mackay

You may be asking yourself the excellent question of why I am talking about asking for help when this book is about forgiveness. The reason is that sometimes we can't completely forgive someone without some kind of help. But help seldom comes if we don't ask for it, so it is important that you discover how willing you are to ask for help. If, while working though one of the forgiveness methods described in Chapter 8, you get stuck on some particular aspect of forgiving someone, that is when you might need to ask for help, and you won't ask for it if you are unwilling to do so.

Asking for help can be especially hard when we are hurting. We may not see the gifts being offered that we can use to heal. Instead, we hold onto our pain. Hence, this chapter.

The principles in this chapter can apply to anything you need help for, not just forgiveness.

Help is a Bad Word to Many People

Because "help" (along with "responsibility") is a bad word to many in today's society, a lot of us have trouble asking for help. We might think that it is shameful to ask for help because we think it is a sign of weakness or failure, or we are afraid people will think less of us. We might believe we have to tough things out and get through whatever problem we are having on our own. Or we may believe we have no difficulty asking for help, but we seldom ask. Sometimes we've learned that help comes at a cost, a cost that is too high to pay—because we end up having to continue to repay the help at a price that is far more than the original help was worth. (Such as emotionally, or in terms of demands on our time or other resources.) Or we think that help is a one-way, dead-end street.

The truth is, as human beings, we are part of a vast social network of other human beings, and we are also all part of the complex, interconnected web of life on this planet. By our very construction, we are not meant to be isolated or to try to survive on our own. We need to interact with our fellow human beings. Helping each other is part of our nature, and we are part of a network of people helping people. Somewhere, people are creating the food and clothing and other physical goods that we need for our well-being and survival, and we in turn are working to earn money so we can purchase what we need, which means we are recompensing them for their hard work. Or we are creating items that can improve the lives of others.

As another way of helping, scientists are researching climate change, food and energy production, medical problems, and other problems of the world, bringing information to everyone so we can all make more informed choices about how we live upon this planet. Sometimes our taxes pay for this research, and sometimes a private company sells the results of that research to help pay for their work. You may argue that if you are paying for it with money, then it isn't help, but the exchange of one thing for another is part of the give and take that keeps life balanced.

Balance is important to the health of our social interactions. It isn't balanced or healthy if one person or group does all the giving and another does all the taking. We all need a healthy amount of give and take in our relationships at all levels, from the individual to the societal. The way human societies are constructed, we use money as a shortcut to keep that balance; we use it to give value for value. Yet the fact that something is exchanged in response to something being given doesn't in any way lessen the value of that which was given.

I'll use a concrete example. Let's say a friend has loaned you a truck that you need to haul something large. This is very helpful; you have the truck available immediately and you don't have to pay for a rental. And of course, to thank your friend, you make sure you clean the truck bed and fill up the tank after you use the truck. Cleaning the truck bed and filling up the tank is courteous and helps keep the balance, but doesn't lessen in any way the value of the help your friend gave in loaning you the truck in the first place. Nor would most people find it shameful or intimidating to borrow a truck from their friends. It's a simple, straightforward transaction—something easily asked for and easily given.

Asking for help in other areas of our life should be as easy and straightforward as that.

Help is Always Available

Help is always available however you choose to view it—whether you believe in a greater spiritual world or gods and goddesses or angels or other such beings, or whether you prefer to believe that the only help there is comes from our fellow human beings or nature or chance.

If you find that this is true for yourself—that you are unwilling to ask for help—explore that aspect of yourself to help yourself overcome that unwillingness. You can think about it, write about it, talk with trusted friends and family members, read books about it, see a good counselor, maybe explore your childhood or family history—there are many ways in which you can look into yourself to discover what holds you back from asking for help. If at first you don't want to talk with someone about it, you have many other resources at hand. A quick search of the Internet or a tour of your local library will show just how much information is available to you. (Just be sensible about the information you find and use judgment and discernment to filter out the bad from the good. Not everything you read on the Internet is true or good.)

Once you discover why you are reluctant to ask for help, you can then work on learning to ask for and accept help. Start small, asking for things that cost little to either party, and pay attention to how you feel when you ask and when you receive. As you become more comfortable with asking for help, you can move to bigger things. As you learn, you'll learn healthy ways to ask for help. For example, it isn't appropriate to try to coerce someone into helping you through guilt.

Learn to Ask for Help

Learning to ask for help has greater ramifications than making the forgiveness process easier. It reconnects you with the rest of the world, putting you more firmly within that framework of give and take that is life. It can improve your relationships and help you avoid the feelings of resentment that can arise when you suffer silently, doing something you don't want to do or that you feel someone else should help you do. Moving away from resentment improves your sense of health and well-being, which can only make your life and the lives of those around you better. For what you are feeling affects how you speak with and act toward others around you.

In addition to asking for help from other people, be open to mentally asking for help. Because this gets into the area of spiritual and religious beliefs, and the notion of prayer, I won't talk about this much. If you have any such beliefs, then act upon those beliefs and request help for whatever problem you are facing in whatever way seems right.

Help Can Come in Unexpected Ways

Once we ask for help, it can come in unexpected ways, and at no cost to us.

Sometimes, when we have a particularly difficult problem to work on, help might come to us in a form that makes it a little easier for us to accept or to heal from things that have injured us.

Here's a personal example. After years of anger toward someone who had deliberately done great injury to me over a period of time, I decided that I was finally willing to let go of that anger, so I mentally asked for help in the matter. Shortly afterward, I had a dream in which that person was arrested and put away for the crimes committed against me. When I woke up from this dream, I had a deep sense of healing and reintegration.

I believe that that deep healing took place with help. I believe that there were spiritual agents helping me, and they were conveying their help through the dream state, so that I would be more able to receive that help at a deep level. Yet even if I only believed that the dream arose out of my unconscious mind, the end result—the healing and forgiveness—was the same.

Likewise, help can come to any of us in dreams, or as a casual remark that we overhear, or as someone saying the same thing to us that others have said, but in a way in which we are able to truly hear the message. We might hear something on the radio, or see a billboard, or see something in nature, or watch a movie and find that the theme is exactly what we are working on ourselves. All these things are help that is coming our way. Whether we choose to hear the message and act on it is up to us. If we aren't paying attention, we can be tempted to think that we didn't get help, and that we solved our problem on our own. It can be easy to dismiss subtle help as insignificant or nonexistent.

For example, let's say you are struggling with an issue you are having with a family member, friend, or other loved one. While you are trying to understand and reach a resolution, you pick up a book and read a phrase from it that exactly addresses the issue, and you gain a sudden insight into the situation. Or you overhear a conversation between two nearby strangers that pertains to and illuminates your issue, or you go see a movie whose theme, it turns out, is the issue you are struggling with. You then use the new information to resolve the issue.

It's Easy to Dismiss Help—But Resist That Impulse

Although it may seem obvious to others that the help you needed was given to you, from your perspective, it can be so easy to dismiss the insight you gained from that book, conversation, or movie as co-incidental and therefore not significant, and to attribute your insight to yourself alone. But when you do that, you are ignoring the fact that you received help that didn't harm you or come with a price tag. And so you continue to be reluctant to ask for help, and to believe that you won't receive it if you ask for it.

I encourage you to start noticing when help comes to you, even when you didn't ask for it, and to acknowledge that the help did, indeed, come to you. And as a next step, I encourage you to be open to asking for help from appropriate, trusted sources. By "appropriate," I mean sources who have the ability to help and of whom it is okay to ask for help. And by "trusted," I mean sources that you are confident will not hurt you either for asking for help or when giving the help that you have asked for.

If you are worried that someone will think less of you for asking for help, remind yourself that it takes strength to ask for and receive help, and that what others think of you in this regard is neither something you can control nor something that you should concern yourself with. If someone thinks less of you, that is their failing, not yours. And do you want to let your fear of what others think of you dictate your actions and happiness?

So while working on forgiveness, be open to asking for help at any time in any form that makes sense to you.

When to Seek Help

You may be in a situation that is beyond the scope of this book to discuss. Perhaps you are in a dangerous situation, or are threatened at work by your manager or coworkers. Although you might find it useful to apply the techniques of forgiveness to the situation, your first concern is to get yourself out of that situation. If someone is abusing you, whether verbally or emotionally or physically, you need to remove yourself from that situation as quickly and as safely as possible.

This is especially true if there are children involved. For your safety and that of the children, seek help immediately. Find a trusted friend or family member or a shelter if you have no other place to go, and also seek a professional who can talk with you about the situation, who can help you understand the dangers, who can get you into a safe place, and who can help you come to terms with the situation so that you understand what's going on and can learn to recognize the danger signs in the future, long before they become a threat to your safety.

If it is a work situation, consult with someone in your human resources department. Harassment in the workplace is illegal in many states (though there are specific laws spelling out what is and isn't harassment), and a good human resources person will not want to see it going on even if whatever is happening doesn't fall under the legal definition of harassment. In any case, you can't be happy when you are being harassed, and it is bound to affect your work performance as well. If there's nothing your human resources person can do, or if your human resources department is not helpful, you may well need to find a new job.

In any of these cases, I encourage you to ask for help from whatever higher powers you believe in, but I also urge you to seek safe human help.

You may also be having a hard time forgiving someone, or dealing with the feelings that are coming up in regard to the person or situation you are forgiving. I talk more about this in a later chapter.

Chapter 7

Who Do You Want To Forgive?

To prepare for forgiveness, make a list of all those people and situations you need to forgive. This list is created using both your gut instincts and your mind, and will be used when deciding who to forgive.

"Lists are a form of power."
A.S. Byatt, The Virgin in the Garden

This chapter is the official start of the core of this book: how to forgive. You might have jumped straight to this chapter because you are understandably in a hurry to get to and through the process of forgiveness, and you might be thinking that all the foregoing chapters contain supplementary material.

Perhaps you expect me to tell you to go back and read everything I've already said. But I'm not going to. I think it can be very helpful to read what I've written; otherwise I wouldn't have wasted my time and yours in writing it. But the purpose of this book is to help you reach the sense of release and peace that forgiveness brings, and it won't help you reach peace to tell you to do something you don't want to do. Your eagerness to get to the point is a good sign; it says that you have the necessary willingness to forgive.

Having said that, I do encourage you to read the earlier sections, because there are many sound, excellent ideas in those chapters that can help you in the process, ideas that lay the groundwork for these techniques. And also, ideas that lay the groundwork for living and thinking in such a way that you eventually won't need these techniques. But if you want to jump right into the process, then certainly do so. However you choose to follow the path toward forgiveness, that is your path, and I am not going to interfere with it by trying to make you feel bad about choosing to do things your way. You can always go back later and read those earlier chapters.

So how do you go about forgiving? What, exactly, are the concrete steps you can take? There isn't just one method, there are many. In this book, I talk about two methods I've developed and refined over the years. The first method, which is a three-step method, takes the least amount of time to complete, but the most work. The other method, which I call the epiphany method, can take more time but takes less effort. You can use either or both as seems fit; for one situation, you may feel that one process of forgiveness is more apt, while for another, you might prefer to use a different process. Or you can apply both methods to one person or situation.

Create Three Lists

But before you move on to reading about the two methods for forgiveness, I'm going to ask you to make three lists. As you make these lists, you'll create the first using your gut and the second using your mind. The third list will be a synthesis of the first two. You will need that final list as a starting point for forgiving.

List 1: The Gut List

For the first list, quickly write down the names of everyone for whom you have feelings of unforgiveness. Do this from your gut, creating this list as swiftly as you can, without a lot of thought. Go on your feelings and your intuition. Don't spend time on any one person or event, and don't write out any details—that will come later. For now, just create a list with very brief entries—a name, or perhaps a word or phrase representing a situation. Use these pointers when creating this list:

- Write down every name and event that occurs to you.
- Don't censor yourself while writing this list.

- Don't make excuses for people who come to mind, or leave them off the list, thinking that perhaps they weren't so bad after all.

Don't worry about the size of the list; just add everyone and every situation and event. as quickly as possible.

List 2: The Mind List

Once you have created this list, now create a second list of people and events you want to forgive. This time, take your time. Use your mind rather than your gut. Write down all the people and events that you find yourself thinking about with discomfort. You will undoubtedly write down many of the same names and events as you did when writing the speed list, but you may also find that you are adding new names or events that are not on the first list (or possibly omitting names that went on your first list). That's okay, and you'll understand why in a minute. Again, keep each entry brief and to the point; now is not the time to get into details.

While creating this second list, you may find yourself wondering about certain people. You may be wondering whether you need to forgive them, or whether what you are feeling will pass without having to work on forgiving that person. You might not need to. It could be you just need to feel and (safely and healthily) express your hurt or anger, and then it is over. However, if the hurt or anger linger, if they last long after the fact of the event, then you most likely need to forgive the situation, person, or thing. So add their names to this list.

List 3: The Master List

When you are done, create a third list from the two lists.

1. At the top of this new list, place all the names and events that appear on both lists.
2. Draw a line under the last name on that part.

3.   Below that line, add the remaining names from the other two lists.

The names above the line on this third list are those people and events that have affected you the most deeply; these have the highest intensity for you.

You may be dismayed at how long your final list is, or even at how long just your high-intensity list is. Whatever length your final list is, is okay. You spent your entire life accumulating the entries on this list; it will take a bit of time to remove entries.

The good news is that you are starting on the process of forgiving those people. You don't need to forgive everyone on your list at once; you just need to get started. More good news is that, the more you practice the techniques given in this book, the shorter your list will become. Even more good news is that, the more you forgive, and the more you practice the techniques in the chapter on changing your thinking (as described in Chapter 4), the fewer people you will be adding to your list. You might not ever add any, or if you do add more, you will be adding names and events at a much slower rate.

If you are feeling a bit overwhelmed at the length of your lists, try this: beside each name, situation, or incident, write the words "mild," "medium," "difficult," or "severe." Then, as you begin choosing people people or situations to forgive, you can start with the mild or medium names first so that you can forgive that person or situation and remove him, her, or it from your list. You'll remove people more quickly from your list that way, which can give you encouragement and confidence to tackle the harder cases.

As a special note, if you did not put yourself on any of these lists, consider doing so. We have all done things that we find hard to forgive ourselves for; the processes in this book are just as valid for forgiving yourself as for forgiving others. (Though I have a separate chapter, Chapter 12, on forgiving yourself.)

Now that you have your master list, you are ready to use the techniques presented in this book to forgive people and events on those lists.

Chapter 8

Forgiveness in Three Simple Steps

Be open to the possibility of forgiveness. With this systematic approach to examining a person or situation, reviewing what happened, and finding new ways to think about it, you can find peace and a release from all those thoughts and feelings that have been bothering you.

"Calamitas virtutis occasio est.
(Calamity is virtue's opportunity.)"
Seneca (Lucius Annaeus Seneca),
De Procidentia *(IV)*

In this chapter, you'll discover my three-step method of forgiveness. At a high level, the three steps (which I describe in detail in the rest of this chapter) are

1. From your master list of people or situations to forgive (which you created in the previous chapter), choose a person, group, or event you are willing to forgive.

2. Create a narrative describing the situation—everything that happened that upset you, saddened you, angered you; everything that you are holding onto.

3. Look at the situation with fresh eyes and find new ways of looking at it, so that you can release your feelings and forgive the person(s) or situation.

It sounds simple, and it is. And it sounds like it can be easy, and sometimes it will be, but it won't always be. Forgiveness is always simple, but it isn't always easy, especially if you are starting the process of forgiveness.

As described in Chapter 4, forgiveness can become a habit of not judging in the first place so that you don't acquire another thing to forgive. Those habits of thinking described in that chapter can also be applied when forgiving someone.

As you apply the three steps to each person on your list, these methods start to become second nature. Each time you use the three steps on someone, you'll further integrate the principles of forgiveness into your life, so that when something happens, right away you'll find yourself using some of your new ways of thinking.

These internal changes can help keep a remark or an event or something someone does from becoming something that embeds in you like a thorn and sticks with you for hours, days, weeks, or even months or years. That way, you accumulate fewer people to forgive, and live a happier, freer life.

Because this three-step method involves writing your thoughts and feelings in a specific way, it works well for many people. But it won't suit some of you. In my experience, some people just don't like to write about their feelings, or just don't like to write, or they can't write. If you are able to write, I encourage you to try this method, because the process of writing helps you connect to deeper thoughts and emotions and awarenesses. But if writing doesn't suit you, then don't feel you have to approach forgiveness in that way. You may be able to adapt these methods by using a voice recorder for each step, for example, or you can use the epiphany method of forgiveness described in Chapter 9; that methods doesn't require writing.

Also, as you embark on this journey of forgiveness, you may find you are only able to forgive part of what someone did, or some aspects of a situation, but not all of it. But that's great! That's progress. That means that to that extent, you have let go of the pain or resentment or anger or other feelings that come with not forgiving someone.

Some Notes Before We Start

Here are some things to keep in mind as you embark on your journey of forgiveness. There will be some things that you'll want to forgive that you'll find easy to forgive. There will also be some things you want to forgive that you can't easily forgive right now.

And there will be some things that you don't want to forgive—at least not right now.

Just tackle the easier ones first, and you'll eventually be able to forgive even the toughest situation. And remind yourself that "no" doesn't mean "no forever"; it just means "no" in this moment. If you are telling yourself, "No, I don't want to forgive that person," add the phrase "at this moment" to the end of that statement to remind yourself that you will eventually be ready to forgive them.

Also, as I said earlier: forgiving someone won't always heal the harm they did to you. For example, if you experienced a great deal of abuse as a child, you may have decided, sometimes at a very deep level, that you are not worth much as a human being. Forgiving the abuser won't necessarily change that belief about yourself. (It can, though.) It will, however, help you clear out a lot of the hurt so that you will be able to tackle that belief and any other core issues arising out of those experiences.

Another note before you begin: don't wait for the person you are feeling unforgiving toward to come to you and ask for forgiveness. They may never. They might not believe that what they did was wrong, or they might not know anything happened at all. Or they might be unwilling to admit that they harmed someone else. So it is up to you to find it in your heart to release the pain.

Your Situation Is Yours; Honor It

This may sound counter-intuitive, but as you practice these methods of forgiveness, don't compare your situation with anyone else's. Don't say to yourself that "things could have been worse." In the book, Little People: Learning to See the World Through My Daughter's Eyes, Dan Kennedy, the author, writes of his family's experiences with their daughter Becky's dwarfism. He spends many chapters on how ill their daughter was her first few years of life, and the many challenges he and his family faced both because of Becky's physical differences and also because of her illness. Yet, he says, it would have diminished what they went through if they were to have said, "It could have been worse." As he says, "What we went through was what we went through. The fact that babies are born with fatal illnesses, that kids are paralyzed in diving accidents, or, for that matter, that families sell their daughters into prostitution on the streets of Calcutta doesn't change any of that. It dishonors Becky and trivializes what was genuinely a traumatic time in our lives to dismiss it by saying, 'well, it could have been a lot worse.'"

So don't diminish the power and effect of your experiences. Yes, others may have been or are experiencing something that in your eyes, by comparison, is far worse. But what you experienced is yours. The pain is yours. You have had to deal with the pain and the consequences since the event happened. Honor yourself by acknowledging how hard it has been for you, even if you are inclined to dismiss it. Not allowing yourself to see how much pain you have experienced is a form of denial, and denial is a way of withdrawing from reality. One important aspect of forgiveness is that it involves facing and embracing your reality so that it is no longer causing you pain.

Working Against Your Nature

Keep in mind that some people will find it easier to forgive than others. Whether we find it easier to forgive depends on how we have shaped ourselves to this point; if we have made it a habit to hold on to wrongs done to us, or to insist on being right, it will be harder to forgive. If we already practice some or all of the principles in Chapter 4, then it will be easier.

But that doesn't mean that you can't forgive if you naturally tend toward being less forgiving. It just means you have to work harder. The good news is, if you know you will have to work harder, and you still apply yourself to forgiving, that means good things about you. It means you are willing to make the world and your own life better by working to change what you have been taught or how you have been raised.

What If It Becomes Overwhelming?

If, when working on forgiving someone, you find that the forgivingness process seems to be spiraling out of control, rein it in. Narrow your scope. Focus on just the person you originally chose, or just one thing that person did, and set the other aspects of that project aside. Then take those aspects that you are setting aside and add them to your list of people and situations to forgive; that way, you know that you will later approach forgiving those other aspects.

Dealing With Difficult Feelings

As I've mentioned before, this book isn't about resolving long-standing emotional issues. Although some of that will come about in the process of forgiving people, the core issues that inform your life are not the focus of this book. Those core issues will have led to the situations that have most profoundly affected you, and those situations have perhaps led to you being in the position of needing to forgive someone.

For instance, if you were abused as a child by your parents or others, one aspect of healing that abuse is definitely forgiveness, but that isn't the only aspect. There are other areas to explore: your mind, your emotions, and your body, for example. There are other aspects of your life and your thinking that require attention to heal the harm. Forgiveness is a part of this, but not the whole. If the harm was severe, then seek a good counselor or read some of the many excellent books on the topic.

But one of the pieces of advice I can give is this: when you are faced with feelings such as panic, anguish, fear, resentment, and doubt, it can be helpful to take a few minutes to breathe. Just breathe in and breathe out a few times: slow, deep, calming breaths. And as you breathe, imagine that you are breathing in calmness and sanity and safety, and that you are breathing out the panic, the fear, the worry, the doubt. Even in an emergency, taking a few calming breaths can help you respond in a better way.

This process of breathing can stand you in good stead in many situations. I say "can" and not "will" because it is up to you. All of this: everything in this book, all of life is up to you. There are many things that can help you, but only the ones that you allow to help you will be helpful. You can relax by breathing, but only if you allow yourself to.

Unfinished Business

Sometimes you have unfinished business with someone. It isn't necessarily bad, but you just have an uncomfortable feeling that something is missing or incomplete. That unfinished business isn't necessarily a need for forgiveness. It could just be that you need to talk something over with them.

Taking care of that unfinished business can be as simple as just calling them or meeting with them to talk about it. But if that person is no longer available to talk with (for example, if they have moved and you don't know how to contact them, or if they have died), then you can still work on resolving those feelings of incompleteness. After all, what you are feeling is inside yourself; therefore, you have full access to all the tools at hand to work with those feelings. In this case, you can use your imagination to imagine yourself sitting down somewhere calm and comfortable with that person, and having a conversation with them. For more information on using your imagination to hold such a conversation, see page X.

Step 1: Choose Someone to Forgive

The first step to forgiving a person, group, or situation is to identify who or what you are willing to forgive.

For this first step, if this is your first time using this method of forgiveness, you may be anxious to jump right into forgiving someone or some situation that really bothers you (perhaps someone from the high-intensity part of your list). But I recommend you set that person or situation aside and instead choose someone you think will be easy to forgive, someone who is on the lower-intensity portion of the list you created in Chapter 7. The second and consequent times you use this process, continue to select people from the lower-intensity part of your list. Then, once you have removed several people from that list, try choosing someone from the high-intensity section of your list.

Here are a few guidelines for choosing someone to forgive:

- Choose only one person.
- Choose someone you are willing to forgive.
- Choose someone you think you will find it easier to forgive.

Choose One Person

When choosing someone from your list, focus on one person, group, or event at a time. Why just one? In the process of forgiving even one aspect of your life, even one group or person, you can discover a complicated web of connections and interconnections with other people and events in your life. It might also prove to be more difficult for you to forgive that person than you anticipate. So it's best to keep it simple and tackle one person at a time. Trying to untangle the connections among all of the different events (or people or groups) that you want to forgive at once would be very difficult.

Choose Someone You Are Willing to Forgive

When you pick someone, ask yourself whether you are willing to forgive that person, group, or event. Are you ready to let the feelings you have about that person or situation change for the better? Are you ready to move on? If you're not ready, it's going to be an uphill battle to forgive. You can still go through the process, but it could be discouraging to you if you don't get the results you are hoping for or that you expect, and you might not get those results if you aren't ready.

Your willingness to forgive is the first key to forgiveness. As discussed in Chapter 5, you need to be willing to forgive before you can forgive. It may sound obvious, but without willingness, you just won't want to forgive that person. If you find yourself unwilling to forgive one person, choose a different person or event that you are more willing to forgive. It won't be productive to try to forgive someone or something when you aren't willing to do so.

When choosing someone to forgive, you might not be willing to forgive everything. But if you can find it in your heart to pick even one aspect of that situation to forgive, then do so.

Finding Willingness Can Be Hard

When you settle on someone to forgive, and start the process of deciding to be willing to forgive them, you may find, even for the "easiest" person or situation, that you are having a hard time finding even a little bit of willingness to forgive that person.

Finding the willingness may well be the hardest part of the process. Asking yourself to consider being willing to forgive someone who has caused you pain can stir up a lot of things you thought you had forgotten. Waves of thoughts and emotions can come at you, telling you all the reasons why you shouldn't forgive this person. It can be overwhelming. You might find that you are angry all over again, or fearful, or sad. Do your best to allow those thoughts and feelings to wash over you. Tell yourself that the fastest way to the other side of those emotions is to go through them. And do your best to look objectively at everything you are experiencing. Ask yourself questions about the thoughts and feelings that are coming up. You might find yourself led to a truth or truths about yourself—possibly truths that you didn't know but are glad to discover now, or possibly truths that you would rather not have known. Don't judge yourself for anything you discover about yourself—although you can't change who you have been or what you've done in the past, there is nothing you can't change about yourself right now. Becoming aware of those things is the first step. Armed with new knowledge about yourself, you can change your thoughts and actions now.

You may discover that the reason you are unwilling to forgive someone is because you think that by holding on to your judgment about him or her being wrong, you are holding them accountable for having been wrong. You might fear that if you think that somehow they aren't wrong about what they did, then you are giving that person, and the world, your agreement for such actions to have taken place, or to continue taking place. Or you may fear that if that person finds out you have forgiven them, they will feel a sense of triumph over you, or worse yet, they will feel that they can continue to treat you badly (if they are still in your life).

We Have No Control Over Anyone Else

The truth is that you have no control over anyone else in this world. Nobody does. Out of fear, people may be doing things at the behest of others that they don't want to do, but it is just that—fear—and none of us need give way to fear and let fear ruin our lives or the lives of others through our own actions. So if you are holding onto the idea that you cannot forgive this person because something bad will happen, you are only holding yourself back, not that other person.

Being willing to forgive someone has incredible healing power. Once you have found it in your heart to be willing to forgive someone—and remember, just a little willingness is all that is required— arriving at that emotional and mental state in which you are willing to forgive that person can itself free you from many of the feelings that were affecting you, and can reduce the strength of those feelings

Choose Someone Who Will Be Easier to Forgive

This is why I recommend that you choose someone or something simpler to forgive, perhaps an event or person that you don't feel strongly about, rather than someone whom you are not ready to work on, especially if this is your very first use of the methods in this book. If you find yourself shying away from a name or situation on your list, or find yourself unwilling to forgive that person, don't start there. That person may well end up being one of your hardest cases; save them for when you have more experience and success with the process. (Though you may be surprised at how easily you'll be able to forgive some people.) Instead, choose someone about whom you feel only a little reluctance to forgive, or for whom you don't hold a large amount of uncomfortable feelings.

Be aware, though, that what might seem like an easy person or situation to forgive can turn out to have deep roots and many branches; forgiving that person or siuation might involve more than you anticipated, and might touch more aspects of your life and feelings than you thought. It might also reach out and pull in other people and situations.

What If It Becomes Difficult?

If you find you have chosen a knotty case once you are into the process, and you are finding it to be challenging, I recommend that you stick with the method, but narrow your focus to just one aspect of the situation. You might not be able to forgive all aspects of that person or situation. That's okay. One reason for sticking with it is, any progress you make toward relieving yourself of the associated uncomfortable feelings is progress toward a happier, healthier life for you. Another reason for sticking with it is, if you give up on your very first foray into forgiveness, you may judge yourself as inadequate to the task of forgiving, and you may find it harder to pick up the process again. So choose carefully, but also tell yourself that whoever or whatever you choose is the perfect choice for you in this moment.

However, if you find you are truly blocked, set this person or situation aside and choose another.

If you decide to ignore my recommendation to choose something easier to start with (which is your right!), just be aware that if you choose to work on forgiving someone who hurt you deeply, or a situation you have been hurting over for a long time, the process can take longer, sometimes a lot longer. You may find that you just can't reach a sense of peace about some aspects of the situation. And you may become discouraged about ever being able to forgive anyone.

If this happens, do what you can in the moment with the resources and tools you have at hand, and set aside whatever needs to be set aside as something to work on later. You may be able to forgive some aspects of the situation, which is progress. And you may plant some seeds that may later sprout and bear fruit in unexpected ways. Just don't let yourself give up if a project proves tougher and more daunting than you expected. If you aren't making any progress, set it aside for a while and choose an easier person or situation to forgive, so you can succeed at forgiving someone. Then return to the tougher situation later.

If you wish to forgive a parent (or parents) or another family member, please read Chapter 12. Our relationships with family members are special and require deeper work.

Benefits of Following This Advice

If you follow this advice: choose one person, choose someone you are willing to forgive, and choose someone you think will be easier to forgive, you should find that the rest of the process goes smoothly. Completing a forgiveness project without large difficulties will give you a satisfying success, which can help in many ways.

- You'll become more familiar with how this forgiveness method works, making it easier to forgive the next person on your list.
- You'll have more confidence in your ability to forgive. Small successes lay the foundations for large ones; the more confidence you have in your ability to forgive, the more easily you will be able to forgive.
- And, of course, you will have better feelings for yourself and one more person in your life; to whatever extent you were able to forgive that person, you'll no longer be carrying that burden of unresolved feelings.

Step 2: Create a Narrative

Once you have decided on a person, and have decided that you are willing to forgive this person (or a situation or event), you are ready for Step 2. In this step, write out everything about the person or what happened that upset you, saddened you, angered you--everything.

I recommend that you write this narrative by hand, rather than typing it. There is something visceral and immediate in writing by hand. There's a connection directly to our hearts and emotions that is harder to access when we are typing. When we write by hand, we can connect more deeply with our emotions and with those aspects of a situation that we didn't realize were there.

Writing things down like this is also essential to the three=step method. It helps you access every aspect of the event or situation, and works well for many people. If the thought of writing down every-thing is daunting, I encourage you to give it a try anyway. There is no alternative that has the same effect as writing down everything that happened, and creating this narrative is essential to the forgiveness process. However, if you just can't do it, then try the epiphany method discussed later in this book.

As you write about the situation, write it as though you are telling the story to someone, or as though you are writing a letter to the person or group involved. But note you will never, ever share that letter with anyone. Because you will never be sharing this narrative with anyone, you can be completely honest about the situation and your thoughts and reactions to it.

This narrative is purely and simply for yourself. You are doing it so you can get a handle on the situation in as complete a way as possible. You won't have to worry about what someone would think, or temper your language, or be diplomatic--nothing of that sort. In-stead, this narrative is for you to thoroughly explore the situation as you experienced it. It is to help you reconnect with everything that happened and to perhaps discover new aspects of the situation that you have forgotten on the conscious level, but that are still there in your heart and soul, affecting everything since that event happened.

Therefore, while on this step, don't censor yourself. Write down anything and everything about the situation that comes to mind. Be as thorough and as angry or hurt as you want. Give yourself as long as it takes to write and feel everything. Do this in a safe, private place.

It can help to pretend you have been asked to give testimony in a court of law. Every aspect of the situation must be reported in order for the judge and jury to make a fair decision. Don't hold anything back. Don't explain or make excuses for anyone, either yourself or any others. Don't judge yourself for how you are expressing yourself or for how much you are saying. Don't think of how someone else would judge what you are saying, or how they would feel about what you are saying. Just explore everything as fairly and completely as you can. Fully express all the emotions you have about that person and event or events.

While writing, include answers to these questions:

- How old were you?
- Who was involved?
- What happened?
- What was said?
- What were you feeling?
- How did it seem the other people were feeling?
- Did you feel like the person or people involved were trying to deliberately hurt you?
- What were your thoughts then and now?

Also, describe the physical environment.

- Where were you?

- Does that location mean something to you?
- What was going on around you?
- What time of day was it?
- What were the sounds, smells, sights, tastes?

Whatever you can remember, whatever stands out, write that down.

During this process, you may be surprised at how strongly you feel; at how angry you are, or hurt, or otherwise in anguish about something that someone said or did. Be prepared for a lot of emotions to come up, feelings you may think you've forgotten or gotten over. These feelings can be quite intense as you realize more about what happened and how you felt about it. You may find you are far angrier than you realized, or more hurt. That's okay. Think of yourself as being on a surfboard, and think of those feelings as waves. Ride those feelings; don't let them swamp you or get the better of you, but instead let yourself feel the full gamut of emotions that come up. Allow yourself to rage against that person, to cry, to grieve—to go through every emotion associated with the event. Don't tell yourself that you shouldn't be feeling this way or having these feelings or thinking these thoughts. These feelings are the waters you must swim through to reach the island of forgiveness.

As you write, if you are struck by insights (about yourself or the person or the situation), write those down.

Temptation to Tell

As you write your narrative, or right after you've written it, you may find yourself wanting to tell someone else about what you are experiencing—either to confront the person you are forgiving, or to share what you are feeling with a trusted friend or loved one.

Don't do it.

At least, don't do it while you are in the grip of your emotions. You are only on Step 2 of this process, and if you act now on how you are feeling, you may regret it later. If you confront the person you are working on forgiving while you are upset, you may say or do things you will later wish you hadn't.

And if you share what you are feeling with a friend, you may likewise say things that you later wish you hadn't. (And bearing in mind the fact that the only safe way to keep a secret is to never share it.) Also, your feelings may change as you work through the process of forgiving your subject, and a friend's natural impulse is to take your side and to dislike and speak badly of the other person. If you say something now, you may damage a relationship you'll later wish you hadn't. It might be harder for your friend to let go of their negative beliefs about that person than it ultimately is for you.

If you find you are having a hard time not acting on or talking about how you are feeling, try to wait until you finish Step 3. Meanwhile, it can help to take a walk or do some hard physical labor. Physical exercise, such as taking a walk, swimming, doing some yard work, or going to the gym, can be a constructive way of working through emotions. However, your sanity and safety are important: if you find you are being overwhelmed by your thoughts and feelings, consult with a trusted counselor.

Note: because of the body-emotions connection, sometimes when you start exercising after not having done so for a long time, you can find that emotions start to surface that you weren't aware of. If that happens, and you start to feel overwhelmed, don't push yourself. Consult with a trusted counselor or a physician who understands this sort of thing, or get some bodywork to help you deal with those feelings.

Once you have written everything down, let it sit for a few days. Then come back to it and re-read it. Do not delete anything! But fill in anything you hadn't remembered when you first wrote everything down, even if it seems minor. For example, if after first writing your narrative, you remembered that someone was wearing a blue dress, add that detail to your narrative.

When you are satisfied that the narrative is as complete as you can make it, set it aside again (for a few days to a week), then proceed to Step 3. In Step 3, you'll look at the facts a little more objectively. But before you start Step 3, I recommend you photocopy or scan your narrative, because you'll be marking it up, and you might want a clean copy to refer to.

Step 3: Look at the Situation With Fresh Eyes

After letting your narrative sit for a week, you are now ready to begin Step 3. In Step 3, you will

- review your narrative to categorize and organize what happened
- look at the situation with fresh eyes to find new ways of thinking about it
- find a gift in the situation
- Forgive some or all aspects of the person or event
- Take action if needed

It can be helpful to have some pens or highlighters in different colors for this step.

First, a note: do Step 3 without judging yourself or invalidating your feelings then or now. Keep in mind that you are looking at the situation from a new perspective and from a different point in time. You are not the same person as you were when that event took place, and your responses, thoughts, and feelings when the event took place can be expected to be different from what your responses, thoughts, and feelings may be now.

Also, as you read the description of this step, keep in mind that I am not asking you to make excuses for yourself or someone else. That can only promote resentment and is the opposite of forgiveness. This step, Step 3, is not to invalidate what your reactions were at the time; it is instead about finding compassion and understanding without condoning the bad things that happened to you. It is very important to know that you are perfectly entitled to your feelings.

As you work through this step, it can be helpful to remember what Mark Twain said in his autobiography:

"Life does not consist mainly, or even largely, of facts and happenings. It consists mainly of the storm of thoughts that is forever blowing through one's head."

In short, the facts or events that happened aren't as important as what we thought about them; one could even say that what happened is what we thought of it. Because our thinking is what influences how we experience something, if we want to change our experiences, we can change our thoughts.

One final thing to keep in mind as you read through this section: by necessity and for the sake of clarity and organization, I've organized this step into specific actions. Read through this entire step before starting, because you'll be doing many of the tasks simultaneously.

Review Your Narrative

Go through your narrative and look for aspects of the situation that are similar to each other. For example, if throughout the situation, someone was repeatedly disrespectful to you (say, by calling you names), that would count as one aspect of the situation. In other words, take each occurrence of disrespect as part of one thing: being treated with disrespect. Each time you were treated that way in the event does not count as a separate aspect of the event. However, the frequency is important. Go through your entire narrative and circle each occurrence of each of those aspects. If you are using colored pens or highlighters, use a different color for each different type of thing. Perhaps red for physical violence, blue for verbal violence, green for betrayal, etc.

If there are similarities in this situation with things that happen to you repeatedly in your life, circle or highlight those as well, and make a note of that other situation. For example, if you found out that you were the other woman (or other man) in a relationship you thought was monogamous, and that sort of thing has happened to you before, make a note of it.

Your resulting narrative will have circles (or highlights) in many colors.

Now, on a separate piece of paper, make a list of the types of things that happened in the situation. Use a word or brief phrase to categorize each of those types of things. Consolidate similar aspects of the event, and keep aspects that are unique separate. Think of it as separating the event into sub-events. Don't repeat everything you wrote about the event; instead, summarize each aspect in just a few words. For example, if you had told your friend Dana a secret, and then Dana in turn told someone else that secret, you don't need to describe the details again; you've already done so in your narrative. Instead, when making your list, summarize that aspect of the event as "Dana betrayed my trust." If you had later confronted Dana with the fact of the betrayal and Dana had denied it, then that lying is also a betrayal of trust, so you don't need to list that as a separate item. (Unless you see the two as distinct, in which case, by all means do so. Use your instincts and discretion in creating this list.)

The list you create can help bring what happened into objective focus. You may well start to have insights as you make the list, especially if you have already used this process to forgive another person or event. You might start to see patterns in terms of what you have found unforgivable, or what hurts you the most. We all have things that bother us that might not bother someone else. You might also start to realize that you have been experiencing the same or similar patterns, which gives you a place to start in learning what you need to learn about yourself to change these patterns.

Feelings will almost certainly come up as you create the list. If they do, set the list aside for a bit until those feelings settle. Or, if inspired by those feelings, write about them separately. Then pick up your list again and finish creating it.

A New Perspective

Now that you have categorized the aspects of the event, take each piece of what happened. Is there another way you could look at each piece, and at the event or person as a whole? To explore that possibility, ask yourself the following interrelated questions:

- Did you have all the facts? Perhaps someone did something inexplicable, but there was more to know that would make that person's actions more understandable. Can you think of a different, more positive explanation for what happened? Is it possible that you misunderstood what was going on? For example, did you choose to look at something as a deliberate attack when it could have just been someone having a bad day?
- Was harm truly intended? In other words, did you ascribe bad intentions to that person that just weren't there?
- Did you take offense because someone did something differently from how you would have done it?

- Even if the person deliberately meant harm, can you find compassion and understanding for yourself, the situation, and them?

Now let's take a look at these questions in more detail.

All the Facts

We seldom know everything that is going on in any situation. That applies to what people's intentions are, and what they are thinking. Unless a person confesses that they meant to do you harm, you don't know for sure. (And even then, they could be lying about their intentions.) We humans ascribe motives and intentions to others around us all the time, but most of the time, it is really our opinions or guesses that we are stating. Unless we can be inside another person's mind, we rarely know for sure. We don't know what someone else is thinking, and we don't always know what happened to them that day, that month, that year, or in their lives. Most often, even if we think we know them well, there is going to be something about them that we don't know that affects how they think about and respond to situations. Very often, their expectations and assumptions are going to be different from ours, but neither they nor we are aware of that.

When looking at your list, ask yourself these questions. "Do I have all the facts? Did I choose to look at something as a deliberate attack, for example, when it could have just been someone having a bad day? Or could that person have not meant it at all, and is oblivious to the effect they had on me?"

Here's an example of how a misunderstanding can arise from making assumptions. I once read about a man who said that in his family when he was a child, anyone who was ill got fussed over. This fussing involved a lot of activity in the sickroom. Ill members were given large glasses of juice, their pillows were plumped up for them, and they were given plenty of books and comics to read. This man married a woman whose family treated ill family members in just the opposite way: people did not fuss over the ill person, but instead kept the ill family member's room dark and quiet and didn't bring them anything.

The first several times each of these two were ill, they treated each other as they had been treated as a child, thinking that was the best way to show their love. As a result, the man was not pampered as he expected, and the woman was not left alone as she expected. They both grew annoyed with each other, feeling as though the other didn't love them. They both assumed that the other person knew how to treat a sick person lovingly, and that because the other person wasn't treating them that way, the other's actions must be deliberately intended to make them feel bad. It didn't occur to either of them that their childhoods had been different, and that what meant love in one family meant rudeness in the other. They only figured it out after a number of fights, after which she got the alone time she wanted and he got the pampering he wanted.

If the situation you are looking at is of this nature: that someone is or was doing something that was contrary to what you expected, ask yourself whether it is possible that a similar misunderstanding is at the root of the issue. If it isn't too late, or if you haven't already, consider talking with that person to clarify what each of you is expecting. It could be a simple difference in assumptions that, once clarified, can help each of you behave toward the other in more understandable ways.

Here are some other examples of ways in which a misunderstanding can arise from not having all the facts and making assumptions. For example, perhaps a person lashed out at you seemingly at random. You might have assumed it was about you, but it is possible that that person was angry over something not related to you, or grieving over something. Their actions also might have arisen out of who they are or were—they might have habitually been an angry person, so they lashed out at everyone. This doesn't excuse them, but might help you see that what they did and how they did it may have had very little to do with you and everything to do with them.

In other cases, perhaps the fault you attributed to them wasn't there at all. For example, we are all subject to bad driving. Sometimes people cut us off thoughtlessly, or speed in front of us recklessly, or don't use their turn signals. But what if the person who cut you off is rushing to the hospital? Or what if a person's turn signals actually don't work, and they don't know it? If you think of a more innocent reasons for those actions, you can relax a bit and not be so angry. You might even be able to help someone.

Here's one example of assuming a good reason for bad behavior: one time I was dangerously cut off by someone who didn't use his turn signal. It was only because I was alert that I avoided an accident. I decided to make the assumption that the driver hadn't meant to do that, so when we drew up next to each other at the next traffic light, I rolled down my window and gestured for him to do the same. When he rolled down his window and looked at me inquiringly, I told him that his right turn signal wasn't working. He looked genuinely surprised and said effusively, "Thank you, I didn't know. I'll get that fixed right away." Now, it is possible that he wasn't telling the truth, but I prefer to think that I helped him and that he did get it fixed. Who knows? He might have avoided the bother of a fix-it ticket, or, more seriously, avoided an accident from cutting in front of a less-alert driver than I was. And even if he simply hadn't used his turn signal and was driving recklessly, the fact that I gave him the benefit of the doubt and didn't confront him with anger may well have encouraged him to drive more safely from then on.

Apply that same principle of finding a different, more innocent reason for actions to each item on your list. If you can't think of something, let that item sit for a while. Come back to it later. If you still can't find something, move on with the process.

Was Harm Truly Intended?

Remember what I said in Chapter 4 (under "Generosity of Heart") about how we are not all alike, and how we can't assume others are like us? Take a moment to ask yourself if the person you are thinking about might be different from you. If that person did something that seemed inconsiderate, ask yourself whether they might not have known it was an inconsiderate thing to do. Although they did something that seemed thoughtless, or careless, or mean-spirited, they simply might not have been aware of their transgression. Some people just don't know.

In some situations, it is possible that you might have misunderstood what was going on, or you might have looked at a situation with your own personal filters coloring the events. The same principle applies to how other people view you as well. No matter what you do or what your intentions are, some people can take offense at it. Just as you have been able to find alternate explanations for things people have done to you that you took harm from, they, too could learn to do that. But until they do, such people will take harm from what you have done no matter what you say or do, and may respond negatively toward you.

Something else to consider: if the event was not recent, but instead happened long ago, it is possible that the person might have matured and changed. When someone was in our lives, and then moved on, we carry a snapshot of them as they were when we knew them. By "snapshot," I mean we have an image of who we think they were at the time. But life moves on for everyone, and many of us grow through our experiences, and change how we think and act toward others. Considering this, it is quite possible that the person has learned to do better. That person may even regret what they did, but has no way to contact you or make it up to you. (Or lacks the courage to do so.)

So we can't assume that anyone is the same as they were long ago, though of course we can't assume they are not the same, either. But since we don't know, it can help to choose to believe that they have changed, or to believe that there is the possibility that they have changed.

Even if someone deliberately set out to harm you, can you find some compassion in your heart for them? How must a person be feeling about themselves if they allow themselves to hurt others? Is it possible that something terrible was going on in their lives that caused them to lash out at others, or to treat others badly? Again, compassion doesn't excuse them—they are still responsible for their actions—but it can bring relief to your heart.

And even if harm was intended, did something positive come of the situation anyway? (For more on this, see the section on finding the gift in every situation starting on page X.)

Someone Did Something Differently Than Desired

One cause of not forgiving someone is because that person simply did something differently than wanted or expected. They didn't mean harm, they didn't do harm, but some people take exception to what someone else has done because that other person did it differently. The assumption in that case is that if someone does something differently, they're just wrong.

The fact is, there are many different ways to do or accomplish many different things. Some may be more efficient, some may be less, but they all get the job done. Some things done differently get different results, but those results are not necessarily bad. They might be a creatively different way of doing something.

If you find that you are angry at someone or are holding something against someone for this reason, consider whether it is worth your health and well-being to be angry about someone doing something differently than you think they should have. Ask yourself some searching questions.

- Do you think there is only one right way to do things? If so, can you expand your thinking to allow the possibility that there can be more than one way to do something right? Can you think of ways in which something can be done differently and yet still be effective?

- Do you think that people must be like you, and that if they aren't, they are wrong? Do you think it is a challenge to you if someone else does something differently than you think it should be done?

- If you believe there is only one right way to do things, are you afraid that someone doing it differently means that you are the one doing it wrong? Consider being open to the possibility that someone can do something differently than you, or think differently, or have different opinions, and still be right without making you wrong.

- Why does it bother you when someone does something differently than how you want them to do it? Is it about control? Do you want people to do what you want them to do, the way you want them to do it, when you want them to do it? And do you think they are wrong or insubordinate if they don't want to? What are you afraid of, if you let others control themselves?

Considering your answers, can you let go of being angry at that person?

Understanding and Reading People

When looking at the situation with fresh eyes, one thing to consider is whether you "read" the people in the situation clearly. By that, I mean noticing what's going on with them; sensing what their mood is, whether they are upset or sad or happy or neutral; knowing whether they are confused or paying attention; even whether they are telling the truth.

If you are good at reading people, you may also be good at understanding them. Some people read others naturally; they have a knack for it because they are observant, they're flexible, they're adaptable, they pay attention; they take information in and don't make snap judgments. Other people can learn to read people accurately, but they find it harder to do because they tend to have preconceived notions that interfere with noticing what is in front of them, or they make snap judgments that they find hard to change later, even if new information comes in that contradicts what they decided. And some people just never learn how to read people.

But reading people is one thing; ascribing motives and intentions to them is another. You may correctly notice a change in mood, say, from neutral to withdrawn or unhappy, but you might not attribute the correct reason. If you are uncertain of yourself or of your relationship with that person, sometimes it can be easy to think that there is something wrong; for example, that they might be upset with you for some reason. But it could well be that the change had nothing to do with you. They might have had a sudden thought that changed their mood.

It might have something to do with you. In that case, that would be something to address. If you trust the person, when you notice a change like that, you could ask, "Hey, it seemed like something changed there. What's going on?" And then talk about whatever comes up.

But when you are remembering a time when you ascribed motives or intentions to someone, it might not be possible to talk with that person about it. In many cases, they may well not remember the event at all, or they may remember it differently. In such cases, when you can't talk with the person about it, try to think of some other reason for that change in mood (or whatever it is you are considering). Did you see something afterwards, or experience something, that seemed like it was a follow-up that would confirm your sense about the situation? Or did nothing happen after that? If nothing happened, there is a good chance that the change you detected had nothing to do with you.

If you are not good at reading people, you might think you are anyway. As I mentioned earlier, we often ascribe to others the same motives and intentions that we have. If we are on the alert for wrongdoing from others, that can mean that we have those motives ourselves.

Here's an example of what I mean. I once knew a woman who hated to be crossed or opposed. It didn't matter how trivial the situation; if another person disagreed with her or inconvenienced her, she took it as a personal attack. She responded to every imagined slight as though someone had actually attacked her, and she actively sought to "get her revenge." Because she was that way, she assumed that others were like that as well, and interpreted their actions in that light. She was always on the alert for threats from others, and saw such threats where none existed. She couldn't see that the actions of others were seldom about her, or that most people didn't mean harm, or that sometimes people were not only innocent of wrong-doing, they actually liked her despite her flaws, and meant her well.

I hope that doesn't describe you, but perhaps you can ask yourself whether that might be what's going on with others around you. Could it be that others are ascribing motives to you that aren't there? Could you be doing the same to others? We are all capable of learning. If you don't think you are good at reading people, that doesn't mean you can't learn to. No matter what we think of our capabilities, it can't hurt to spend a little time studying human nature and personality theories to find out that we are not all the same, and to find out in what ways we are different, and to see how the strengths of different people can complement ours. To that end, I highly recommend studying the Myers-Briggs typology theory, which is based on Carl Jung's theories, which were in turn based on several-thousand-year-old Greek theories of human nature and personality.

Healing the Pattern

If during this process you have realized that you have repeated a pattern in different situations with different people, and if you are just seeing the pattern now, that's one good thing arising out of the process of forgiveness. Seeing a pattern is the first step in being able to change it. It can be helpful to consider that the other people involved were there to help you discover and heal that pattern. I'm not saying they were doing so consciously; just that the situations you were in were giving you the opportunity to realize that you have been living your life repeating certain experiences.

Beyond that realization, you can learn what your underlying motivations were for putting yourself in those situations in the first place. Sometimes we repeat certain types of situations and choose to be with certain types of people because we are trying to heal pain from our childhood. For example, until we resolve our childhood issues, we often choose men or women who are like our parents, and then expect or hope for different things from our relationships with them. (I speak more about forgiving parents and other family members in Chapter 12)

But the people involved in your patterns are not the people you originally took pain from. It is up to you to heal what is within so you don't repeat those patterns. You can start the healing by asking yourself what thoughts or beliefs about yourself, others, and the world you are trying to heal. Does the pattern resemble something from your childhood or earlier life that you took harm from, and that you have since been trying to resolve? If you see a pattern but are at a loss for why you are repeating it, this might be a good time to find a trusted counselor.

Find the Gift

Now that you have reviewed your narrative and have asked yourself some questions, the answers to which have shed a different light on the person and situation, you may already be feeling better about the person or situation. You may have had some insights that have helped you to release some of your old thoughts and feelings concerning that person or event.

One of the first ideas to consider when thinking about forgiveness is that something good for you can arise out of bad things. Another is to know that the pain is never pointless, nor have you wasted your time being angry or hurt and not forgiving people. In the process of forgiveness, you look upon every aspect of your life, and every aspect of things you have taken harm from, with new eyes, with eyes of forgiveness and understanding, so that you feel good—not just good, but great—about yourself, about your life, and about what's happened to you.

Now that might sound bad. You might be asking, "why should I feel great about something bad that happened to me? Is that even possible?" I tell you it is possible. You can get to the point where you see that something good, or many good things, came from what happened. It's been my experience that when it seemed that people were trying to harm me, or when apparently harmful things had come my way, I was either not truly harmed, or the effects I perceived as harm later turned into a greater good for me.

So as a next step, look for the gift or gifts you gained out of the situation, or out of the interaction with the person you are forgiving. You may be asking what I mean by "a gift."

Dan Duggan, a professor at Santa Clara University (which is a highly respected private Jesuit university on the level of Stanford) taught that there is a gift in every situation, even if it seems as though the situation has no redeeming qualities. At the time, I wondered what kind of gift can arise out of a bad situation. In the course of taking his classes, and in later applying his advice, I've learned that the answer is, "Plenty."

The way to find a gift is to examine what happened and look for something good to have come out of it. For example, if you applied for a job and didn't get it, it could well be that the next job you find and take will be much better for you in every way than the job you didn't get. It may pay more, offer more opportunities, have a more pleasant group of people to work with, be a more ethical workplace, involve less of a commute, or in some other way or combination of ways improve your quality of life.

As another example, let's say you dated someone who behaved badly toward you. That person probably had some good qualities, or you wouldn't have been attracted to him or her in the first place. But as your relationship continued, some other qualities came out, qualities that eventually were unacceptable to you, and you ended the relationship. Following the principle of finding the gift, after you end the relationship and before you get into another, you spend some time (possibly months or even years) thinking about the relationship. In thinking it over, you realize that you learned a lot about yourself and what you preferred in a relationship. That's a wonderful gift: from that point forward, you will be able to choose only relationships in which those things that you prefer are present. (This approach of taking some time between relationships is also a good way to make sure you don't take baggage with you into a new relationship.)

To find a gift in the situation, ask yourself what positive thing has come out of what happened. There might be more than one gift in it, but find just one first. By "gift," I don't mean something physical (though it could be that). Instead, I mean something of value that enriches your life in other ways—spiritually, mentally, emotionally, or physically. Think of one good thing that has come to you because of what happened. For example, because of this situation, did you

- Learn something about human nature that will keep you from being hurt that way in the future?
- Learn something new and helpful about yourself, this person, or people in general (for example, something that has helped you to do things differently, or think differently, in healthier ways)?
- Rearrange your life or make different life choices that were better for you?
- Change habits, where the new habits will last a lifetime and enrich your life?
- Experience a change in your circumstances that ultimately ended up with you in a better place, either a new job that is

more satisfying for you, or in a new location that is better than where you were before?

- Gain a friendship?
- Gain one or more new family members whom you cherish?

Initially, it can be pretty hard to find a gift, because you may be blocked by such things as anger, resentment, fear, and judgment. You may not want to give up thinking about the situation in just one way. But remind yourself that you were able to find the willingness to forgive this person or situation. If you need to, review the reasons why you were willing to forgive.

If you can't find a gift, or if you find a gift bu wonder why it had to come to you this way, remember that Mark Twain once said, "If you hold a cat by the tail, you learn things you cannot learn any other way." There are some things you cannot learn any other way than by going through a situation in a particular way. It could be that, whatever situation you are looking at, that situation was the only way you could learn something. If you are having trouble finding the gift in what happened, ask yourself what you have learned, if you haven't already done so.

If you still can't find the gift, you might need to use your imagination to come up with a scenario. Let's look at the job example again. Although you may know that the commute for your new job is less than it would have been for the job you didn't get, you might not know what kind of people you would have been working with, and you may not know what opportunities you would have encountered in the job you didn't get. In this case, creatively imagine ways in which your new job is better than what the other job seemed to offer. You may think you are just making it up, but it could well be true. You may never know whether your new job is worse or better than the other job. Believing that your new job is worse can make you unhappy, so you might as well choose to believe that it is better.

If you can't find a gift, let it sit and come back to it later. Once you find one gift, try finding more. You could make it a fun challenge to see how many separate, distinct gifts you can find in the situation.

The Next Step

After you have worked through the three steps of forgiving some-one, you may well have found complete peace about that person or situation. But if you feel you haven't reached complete forgiveness, there are more things you can try. These are described in the next chapter. Or you might just want to refine the forgiveness process; I make some suggestions on doing so in the next chapter as well.

Also, make this process your own. The process won't work if you don't use it, and if you won't use it because you would like to change some aspect of the process, then make that change. (Though I have good reasons for each step, so I only recommend you make changes within each step; don't eliminate or skip an entire step.) In short, do what you need to do to make forgiving easier for yourself.

Chapter 9

The Next Step

"Trials are but lessons that you failed
to learn presented once again, so where
you made a faulty choice before, you
now can make a better one, and thus
escape all pain that what you chose before
has brought to you."
A Course in Miracles, T-31.VIII.87:1.

After applying the three step process of forgiveness, it is very likely that you will have gained a greater understanding of yourself, the situation, and the people involved. During the process, you may have already forgiven the person or situation, either partially or completely. Even partially is great!

Forgiveness is both a choice and the result of relieving your mind and heart of the burden you have been placing on it with your thoughts and feelings. Having gone through this process of forgiveness, which is a process of healing and integration, if there are still areas in which you feel unhealed, and especially if you still feel a great deal of pain, anger, or other emotions toward someone or some situation; if, in short, you haven't yet forgiven the person (or any aspect of the situation) to any extent, the final, crucial step is to consciously choose to forgive.

This means applying your rational mind and asking yourself to forgive that person or situation. There are other, more complex things that can get in the way of forgiveness, but at the core, willingness is still the key. When you started this process, you had decided you were willing to forgive that person; has that willingness changed? Did going through Step 2 revive old feelings that made it harder to be willing, even after going through Step 3? Perhaps it would be helpful to revisit that willingness and ask yourself again if you are willing to forgive that person or situation. Are you telling yourself reasons why what that person did was still wrong? Are you holding onto your pain for some reason? Find out why. And remember, forgiving someone will heal the emotional pain that you are holding onto—the thoughts and feelings you have been holding against that person—but it won't always heal deep-seated, underlying beliefs about yourself. For that, you will need to seek healing in other ways, such as with a trusted counselor.

If your answer is still "Yes, I am willing to forgive this person," then there are a few more things to try, as described in this chapter. If, after you have tried them all, you still haven't forgiven, then add this person or situation to your "high intensity" list and set him/her/it aside for now. Later, after you have successfully forgiven more people or situations, revisit this person. When you do that, go through the entire three-step process again.

Ten More Things To Do

If, after going through the three-step process, you haven't forgiven the person or situation, and you've revisited your willingness as discussed in the previous section, and you are still willing, but you are still struggling with forgiving the person or situation, here are ten more things to do. You don't have to do them all; use your judgment and inclinations to decide which to try.

- Have a mental conversation with the person you are forgiving.
- Consult with a friend.
- Check in with yourself to make sure you have stayed on target.
- Ask yourself if trust is an issue.
- Ask yourself if you are doing it too.
- Find ten things you like about the person.
- Ask yourself if the problem is that you idealized the person.
- Ask yourself if you are telling yourself that they should have known better.

- Choose to think differently about the people you want to forgive; are you being held back by lingering thoughts or feelings?
- Try the epiphany method described in Chapter 10.

Mental Conversation

One thing you can do to help resolve your feelings about a person is to have a mental conversation with that person. I don't mean connecting with that person by calling them on the phone, sending them a text or email, or anything like that. I mean just sitting quietly and imagining that person is present, then imagining a conversation with that person. When you do this, you can help clear the air, at least for yourself.

Set yourself one or more goals for this conversation, such as reaching some kind of resolution, achieving a new understanding of that person, or hearing from them what you want to hear. One important thing to remember: keep this conversation positive and results-oriented.

In this imagined conversation, you can safely ask them anything you want, or tell them anything you want. Allow yourself to be fair and as objective as possible. Allow that person to give his or her side of the story. Follow through with every line of thought in this conversation, and see where it takes you. If you want to hear them say something, like "I'm sorry," imagine them saying so, even if you don't think they would say it in real life. Wherever you want the conversation to go, take it there.

Although this is just an imaginary conversation, it can be powerfully effective. It is said that the subconscious mind doesn't differentiate between fact and fiction: whatever you experience, even if only verbally or visually, your subconscious mind takes as "real." This is why our hearts pound and our bodies are drenched with sweat and filled with adrenaline when we watch the tense or scary parts of action or horror movies. If some part of us didn't take the movie as real, we would just be watching calmly, with no reaction at all aside from an appreciation for the art of the movie makers.

Likewise, when you imagine something, your subconscious mind takes that as "real" as well. So when you have this mental conversation, your subconscious takes it as the real deal and responds accordingly. This imaginary conversation can therefore set in motion some very real positive results.

Consult with a Friend

Remember how I said in Step 2 not to talk about what you've written? If you are stuck and unable to forgive a person or event, now is a good time to talk about the issue. Sometimes it can be helpful to consult with a friend to hear what they think. To be most effective and useful, that friend should be someone you trust, someone who can be neutral and objective. A friend can offer a new perspective, or perhaps see something you are not aware of in a situation. Make sure you ask your friend if he or she is willing to do this, and, just as with the mental conversation, assure them that you want the conversation to be positive and results-oriented. Or, if you are comfortable with it, seek a trusted counselor to talk it over with. It could be that your friend or counselor will be able to help you see aspects of the situation that you haven't seen before, or can help you differentiate between forgiving the other person and healing yourself.

Are You Still On Target?

Check in with yourself to make sure you have stayed on track in terms of your willingness to forgive this person. Is it possible that you have strayed away from the specific person, event, or situation and gotten bogged down in some other issue? If so, set that other issue aside for now and return to focusing on the main person or event. Or, if it feels right, set aside the main person or event and apply the three steps of forgiveness to the other issue. It could be you need to address that other issue before you can make headway with the initial person or event you chose.

Is Trust an Issue?

When your trust has been damaged, it's tempting to never trust the person who damaged that trust. In many cases, that is the perfectly healthy response. Some people just aren't trustworthy, and it is a case of, "fool me once, shame on you; fool me twice, shame on me." As John F. Kennedy once said, "Forgive your enemies, but never forget their names." Forgiveness is for yourself, to help you heal the harm that was done and to release the harm you continue to do to yourself through your thoughts about the person or situation. But if you forget who did the harm, you won't be on the lookout for a repetition of that harm. In other words, some people just can't be trusted. They meant you harm then, and they'll harm you again if given the chance. One very important thing to remember is this:

You don't have to associate with people you've forgiven.

Some people are just going to wreak havoc no matter what--it's in their nature. So unless you like chaos and harm, you might prefer to stay away from them.

But sometimes whatever happened was out of the ordinary for that person. It wasn't typical of that person. If you decide this is the case, you can also decide to give them another chance and to trust them again; to treat them with innocence, from your point of view, anyway, and an expectation of good. And surprisingly, that can elicit responses that you might not otherwise get.

Am I Doing It Too?

It can be helpful to look at something someone has done and ask yourself, "Is there something about what they did that is similar to something that I do?" (Something you do or did to yourself, or to others, or possibly even to that person.) Do this not to judge yourself, or to make yourself feel bad, but to realize that one of the following (or maybe all) is true:

- Whatever it was is just something that many people do, yourself included, and doesn't arise out of bad intentions.
- Although what that person did was not convenient for you, it is not a punishable offense—it was just not convenient for them to do what you wanted them to do.
- The reason you are so angry about it is that you are angry with yourself for doing it, and are putting that anger out onto someone else. (The technical term for this is projection; you take some part of you that you are not comfortable with and tell yourself it isn't true about you. Instead, you project it, like a movie, onto other people. You see in others that which you dislike in yourself whiteout always realizing what you are doing.)

Ask yourself this question, not for the reason of judging yourself or others, but for the reason of saying, "Hey, this is something everyone does; it's a mistake (or, it isn't optimal), but I can learn from it and not judge them or myself for it" (that's one possibility). Or of saying, "What that person did was inconvenient for me. But it wasn't convenient for them to do what I wanted them to do, and perhaps it was unrealistic of me to expect them to do it."

If it is something you do, or did, that you feel unhappy with yourself about, then this is an opportunity for you to take another look at that, and work on the issue within yourself rather than focus on that issue in others. Becoming more aware of yourself can never be a bad thing.

It is a step in the right direction; you cannot change something you aren't aware you are doing. Once you become aware of it, you can work on changing it without judging or hating yourself.

Ten Things You Like or Admire

If you are struggling with angry or critical or judgmental or resentful thoughts about someone, then here's a simple thing you can do to help change those thoughts. I say "simple," but although the process itself is simple, it can be hard to do. It becomes easier with practice. You can do this any time, not just when in the process of forgiving someone; for example, if you are in the middle of a situation, you can do this to achieve some emotional relief.

Get out a piece of paper and start writing down things about that person that you admire. (You can do this mentally as well.) Chances are, if you are angry, you are going to think, "Oh, I don't admire them at all." But if that person is in your life, there had to have been something about them that you admired initially. (Family members are a special case and I talk about them later in this book.) So try to remember what it was that you admired, and write down those things if you think they are still true. What you write can be as basic as, "They dress nicely" or "They have a pleasant voice."

Give yourself a goal of how many pieces of appreciation you want to come up with (like pieces of flair)—ten? Fifteen? Twenty? If you think those are too many, then give yourself a goal of five things you admire or appreciate about that person. Or even just one. The first one will be the hardest. When you come up with one, think of five. When you think of five, think of two more.

Because you are focusing on the positive, this exercise will lighten your mood. Your body will relax and stop releasing those stress hormones. This exercise can also affect on your relationship with that person. Even if you don't say anything to them about this list, which I don't recommend (i.e., I don't recommend you share the fact that you made this list), something about you, either a slight change in your demeanor or tone of voice, will affect them as well, and they will, in most cases, respond to this positive flow of energy you are sending their way.

An Idealized Person Disappointed You

Sometimes what you need to forgive is not something wrong or bad that someone did, but the fact that you idealized them so much that anything they did that was not perfect has caused you pain.

It is unrealistic to expect anyone to be perfect. We are all human beings, learning to be more fully the ideal human being, but no matter how much of a paragon someone is, few in history, let alone anyone alive today, have reached that state of perfection.

As human beings, we all make mistakes, and often those mistakes affect others negatively. When we idealize someone so that in our minds they can do no wrong, and then they inevitably make a mistake, then our reaction can be pretty harsh. Just think of how vehemently some people respond when a public person (actor, politician, or other leader) comes up short of our expectations or ideals.

If you have idealized someone in your life (teacher, doctor, older sibling, beloved aunt) and you are not forgiving them because they made a mistake or behaved differently than you expected, think about that from a rational perspective. People can have many wonderful qualities, but nonetheless we are all still human; we all make mistakes or disappoint others because we aren't who others want us to be. Often, our anger stems from the fact that we identified with them and were telling ourselves that, if that person was capable of being so perfect, then we were too. When that person fails to be perfect, it arouses fear in us that we can't achieve perfection after all.

Striving for perfection can bring good things, but only if we realize that we all, every one of us, will fall short of perfection, and that doing our best is plenty to expect of ourselves and each other. Insisting on perfection in ourselves and others can paralyze us and make us ineffective in life; some people never complete projects or make decisions because the circumstances aren't perfect.

One idea that can help is that perfection isn't a static state; it is a process of always becoming more. We are all like kittens, who are perfect as kittens, and yet learn more and become more as they grow into cats. So if this is the issue, do your best to let that person be a flawed human being and yet still be acceptable to you.

"They Should Have Known Better"

One of the things that can keep us angry toward someone is thinking that they should have known better, or believing that they did know better, but they did it anyway, and that therefore what they did was unforgivable. After all, as Socrates once remarked, no one needs to be taught what is bad and what is good; we all inherently know it. So if we know that what we are doing is wrong (or bad), and we do it anyway, then what does that say about us? Or what does that say about another person who deliberately does harmful things?

The truth is, even if we all mean well (and I believe that at the core, everyone does want to be helpful and contribute to life), sometimes we get confused and lose sight of the ultimate good that we are all a part of. We get narrowly focused on our individual goals and don't see how the choices we make are harmful to others. We ask ourselves the wrong questions about how to achieve our goals, so that the answers we get are not completely ethical or moral or life-enhancing.

Here's an example of what I mean by asking questions. Let's imagine a company that manufactures a product (it doesn't matter what kind of product). If the company president asks her top managers to think of ways to make the company more profitable, and that is the complete wording of her sentence, she will get answers that don't involve concern for others or the environment. She might get answers such as,

- Use cheaper packaging that isn't made from recycled content.
- Provide less product in each package (a sneaky way to raise the price).
- Use cheaper (shoddier) materials in the product.
- Raise the price on the product without giving anything more in value.
- Lay off people and ask the remaining people to do more work and to work longer hours.
- Reduce wages or benefits.

But if the company president asks her top managers to think of ways to make the company more profitable while continuing to provide a healthy workplace, give good value to the customers, and reduce harm done to the environment, she might get such answers as,

- Reduce the amount of packaging used, which will reduce costs and overall waste, and use recycled or otherwise environmentally sound packaging.
- Reduce waste in the workplace, reuse resources, and recycle within the company.
- Train and educate people and get them engaged and caring about the company so that everyone starts contributing toward the success of the company.
- Make the workplace a better, safer environment to reduce waste and costs.

It's all in what question you ask and how you ask the question. To call on Socrates again, we can learn that the wording of a problem carries within it the seeds of its own solution. If you state the problem one way, you get one set of answers. If you state it another, you get a different set of answers.

This principle applies on the personal level as well. We all have goals, but often we don't get as far as asking ourselves questions about how to reach those goals, and what we will do to surmount obstacles. Sometimes we don't even clarify what our goals are. We just react to life, and so we find ourselves making less optimal or life-supporting decisions. We might not even think about it at the time, but the cost to the quality of life for us and those around us is high. And even if we are aware of the harm we've done, we might tell ourselves that we had no choice or that there was no other way.

But we always have a choice, and there is always another way. If we take a moment to think about what we are doing ("What do I want to do here?"), and why ("Why do I want to do that? Do I even need to do it?"), and how ("How can I accomplish that without doing harm?"), then we will start seeing alternatives where before we thought there were none.

Choose to Think Differently

If you have been in the way of someone's steamroller approach to achieving their own goals, it is tempting to blame them or be angry at them for not taking more care with the feelings of those around them. You might be thinking that they should have known better (as discussed earlier). But as a friend once said to me many years ago, "What should be and what is are two different things." There are just some things you can't change, and you definitely can't change people. An individual is the only person who is in control of himself or herself. Much as you may wish otherwise, it is their life, their choice, and their decision to be that way. You might as well get angry at a cat for purring or a dog for barking or a rooster for crowing. It is in their nature to purr or bark or crow, and unless you put an end to the lives of the cat or dog or rooster (all unacceptable solutions), you are not going to stop that behavior. Likewise, you can't change another person's nature.

Not forgiving someone means holding onto the feelings associated with whatever happened, the anger, the pain, as though somehow that makes us right and the other person wrong. If you are hanging onto something because you are angry at someone, ask yourself, who are you punishing, and why?

Nor should you worry about trying to change someone or stop someone. If someone is harming you, take the appropriate steps to protect yourself (which might mean simply distancing yourself from that person), but don't think you are going to change them. When people are abusive, they are that way because of deep-seated problems that you have no way of healing. They might not even be aware that they are abusive, and even if they are, they are unlikely to stop being that way. Consider the two possibilities: either they have control over their behavior, or they don't. If they have control, then they are being abusive because they enjoy it. If they don't (i.e., if they are acting out unresolved, unhealed psychological or physical harm done to them), then they can't stop themselves from doing it.

People Are Who They Are

Take a look at the shape of this paragraph. It could be formatted any number of ways using different typefaces, different spacing between the lines, and so on. The typeface and shape even affect how people perceive the contents—whether they think the contents are more trustworthy or reliable than if the typeface and shape were different. But that outward appearance doesn't alter the content; the words remain the same.

Just so, people are who they are. We come in many different shapes and sizes, but our individual contents are always what they are for each of us. It is possible that we can change with the help of a spiritual Editor, but that change can take a long time if we have been deeply harmed.

The bottom line is that it is wasted time and energy worrying about how someone is, or blaming them for being the way they are, or thinking they should have known better. If someone truly knows better, either they do harm because they want to, or they did harm inadvertently. If they wanted to hurt you, there's not much you can do about that but forgive them, remember they are hurtful people, and move on. If they do harm because they can't help themselves, then it is up to you to forgive them and remove yourself from their presence.

If they slipped up or made a mistake, then again, what you can do is forgive them and move on with the relationship. No amount of saying that things should have been different is going to make them different.

Feeling Sanctimonious

Sometimes when you think of someone who has done wrong by you, you might feel sanctimonious. I am not advocating feeling bad about yourself when you are feeling sanctimonious, but I do recommend that you move away from that feeling and its attendant thoughts. I recommend that you genuinely and truly find it in your heart, from your perspective, to make allowances for people, to find a different way of looking at things that doesn't judge them or attack them (even if it's just a mental attack on your part), but instead to let them be. Let them be who they are. Let them be as they are.

I think sometimes we want to let people be who they are, but when we've forgiven them, especially for something really hurtful, there can still be that tiny little bit of "gotcha" feeling, of "you've done something wrong and I know you've done something wrong, but I'm a bigger person than you, and I am going to forgive you," or "I am going to say 'yeah, it's okay, but it's okay because you were wrong'" (or some other reason that in itself is an attack).

It's not comfortable feeling that way, but it's sometimes easy to miss the fact that we are feeling that way. This is because we often ignore certain awarenesses about ourselves. We're afraid of facing who we genuinely are. We're afraid, because we think we might be someone different, someone less likable, than we would like to be.

But the more we face who we really are—if we're being sanctimonious, for example—the easier it is to learn how to adjust our thinking, adjust our attitude, change our approach, change our feeling, and then we will be less sanctimonious and we'll like ourselves more. But allowing ourselves to see that we are being that way is a key part of that. We have to first accept that we are something before we can change it.

Feeling Vengeful

As you work on forgiving someone, you might be telling yourself that you forgive someone or you understand them or you know what's going on with them. But if you are still feeling angry or vengeful or self-righteous toward them, or if you are feeling undercurrents of, "I forgave the bastard, and he is going to regret ever harming me as he roasts in hell while I sneer at him from heaven," then your forgiveness isn't complete. You are still carrying a disheartening burden that will color everything you do.

Whether you haven't completely forgiven someone, or whether you aren't entirely sincere about your forgiveness, others will know. They always know, whether they show it or not, whether they let themselves be aware of it consciously or not. They know, and that knowing will affect how they treat you and how they think of you. And how they think of themselves. Which in turn affects how they treat others and think of others, affecting those they know, and so on--rippling out from you in quiet waves, eventually affecting the whole world. And so you affect the peace of the entire world for good or ill by what's in your heart.

If it is comforting to think that the person who harmed you or yours will someday see the error of his ways (or hers), then by all means think that. But if you are also thinking that they will suffer pain when they realize the harm they've done, and you take pleasure from that thought, then you are still holding onto your own pain or anger. So make sure that your heart is clean; any amount of satisfaction at someone else's anticipated suffering is that much separation in your heart from your most loving nature.

Still, to whatever extent you can forgive a person or situation, to that extent you have released yourself from pain and have made your life and the world a better place.

Try the Epiphany Method

If, after all this, you are still having a hard time forgiving someone, then it is time to try the epiphany method, which is described in the next chapter. This method only requires willingness and the intention to forgive; otherwise, it requires very little effort.

Refining Your Process of Forgiveness

As you forgive people, you may start seeing how your reactions in one situation are similar to your reactions in another, different situation, which in turn can lead you to seeing the similarities between those situations—perhaps there are certain things that bother you in particular, and those things are present in both situations or in interactions with both people, however otherwise different those people or situations may seem.

That information in turn can help you see the similarities in yet other situations, and in new situations. In this way you'll gain a greater understanding of yourself, making it more likely that you will be able to respond differently in such situations. You can also gain a greater understanding of human nature, and more specifically of those people who are or have been in your life.

When we understand someone, we find it easier to forgive them. This still doesn't mean condoning what they did or are doing, but when you know what drives someone, you can be less frustrated and confused, which means more centered, which means more able to see with your heart.

Telling Someone You've Forgiven Them

There's a temptation, when you've forgiven someone, to tell them that you've forgiven them. But if the person doesn't think that they did anything wrong, they may take offense, because you are essentially saying to them, "What you did, which you think is fine, I didn't think was fine, but now I've forgiven you for it." (Or worse yet, "What you did that you don't think you did...")

To forestall even having to forgive someone, when you have a problem with someone, try to work it out with them first. Nothing is going to happen if you just sit in silence and suffer. Yes, there are some people who won't want to hear it. They won't listen and they're stuck in their ways; they can't change, they won't change. But for most reasonable people, the first approach is to go talk with them about the issue and see if you can work it out before it escalates. When you do that, you are essentially telling them, "there is a problem here." (Which they might not already know. You may think they know; you may think it is obvious. But what you think is obvious may well not be obvious to others.) When you say this to someone, that person may not agree with you, but at least you've given them the information that there is a problem, and have given them the opportunity to fix it. And even if that person won't listen or change, how are they to know if you don't speak up? Give people the benefit of the doubt and give them the information.

Once they know that there's a problem, if the circumstances change for the better as a result of your conversation (which is great!), you may still need to forgive what has already happened. And if nothing changes, then, to be happier about that person, look inside yourself for what you want to do next to free your heart of pain, resentment, and anger. Once you feel good about the situation, then you may no longer feel the need to tell them that you forgive them.

If, after you have resolved the issue in your heart, you feel sure that someone would like to hear that you have forgiven them, wait a while to make sure of your motivations. Make sure your heart is clean and that you are not going to be rubbing their nose in what they did; make sure you aren't going to be using your forgiveness as a way of triumphing over them or making them wrong.

Once you've let it sit a while, you may find you no longer wish to tell them. You might think you "should," though, but sometimes "should" really means "shouldn't." Deciding whether to tell someone you have forgiven them is a judgment call. Trust your gut over your head on this. It requires a good understanding of human nature and of who you are dealing with. But this book is not about learning how to be a good judge of people, learning how to understand people, and learning how to read the people around you. Those are certainly skills that will help you to be able to respond better in a situation, and help you to know when to tell someone that you're cool with something, and when not to say anything, but they are not the focus of this book. (Though you can start to learn those skills if you practice the ways of thinking that I describe in this book.)

Three Questions To Ask Yourself Before Speaking

If you feel very strongly that you do want to tell someone that you have forgiven them, then run that desire through three filters before acting. (These filters have been around a long time.) Ask yourself (and answer honestly),

1. Is it the truth?
2. Is it kind?
3. Is it necessary to say?

"Is it the truth?" Will what you be saying be true? In the case of forgiveness, if you feel you have truly forgiven someone, then your answer would be "yes." But have you forgiven them for something they did on purpose? If not, it might not be true from their perspective.

"Is it kind?" Can you say it in a truly kind way? Or would it harm the other person to hear what you have to say? Even if it is the truth, would it make them feel better about themselves, or worse? It can't be kind if you are saying something negative about something they have no control over.

"Is it necessary to say?" Does the person you want to say this to really need to hear it? Will it make a positive difference to them or to others around them if you say this? Will something change for the better?

If you are able to answer "yes" to all three questions, and you tell the person, if they respond well, that's great. But don't be surprised if they response negatively anyway. Many people might take it as though you are rubbing their nose in something they can't help.

You may find it useful to apply this set of questions to anything you want to say, not just in the case of forgiveness. It can save everyone a lot of trouble. Some people just aren't ready to face things. For example, some people are not ready to release their pain. Even though they say they don't want to stay in the painful situation, their actions say otherwise; they resist any attempts on the part of others to help them, and reject anything that would give them a solution to their problems (including changing how they are thinking about themselves or their situation). In such cases, saying anything to them about how they are the authors of their own pain might be the truth, but it would not only be unkind, it would also be unnecessary (because it would do no good).

If you decide that saying something doesn't pass these three tests, but you really, really want to say something, write it all out in a letter, but don't ever send that letter. Destroy it after writing it.

Chapter 10

Forgiveness By Epiphany

Forgiveness can come to us as easily as waking up to a spring morning. If we are willing to trust to the inner workings of grace, we don't have to work hard for forgiveness; we don't even have to work at all. I call this forgiveness by epiphany.

"Grace ... transforms a moment
into something better."
Caroline Myss

In addition to the three-step method, I've discovered another method for forgiving someone, which I call forgivenss by epiphany. The three-step method requires a lot of writing and thinking, and some people don't enjoy writing things out—it doesn't appeal to them, or it doesn't work for them, or they physically cannot write. This might be the case for you. Or you might think that the three-step method is too much work—and it *is* a lot of work, but work that is well worth the results.

If this is the case for you, try the epiphany method described in this chapter. The epiphany method can enrich and supplement any other approach to forgiveness, and can be used for any effort at forgiveness that you are making, including yourself.

What Is an Epiphany?

An epiphany is a moment of sudden clarity, insight, and wisdom. It comes seemingly out of the blue as a realization, and brings with it a change (sometimes a radical change) in how you think or feel about something. It can be a personal insight about yourself, or an insight about someone or something else; it can be small or it can be huge. It can be personal, relevant only to you, or it can have global effects. Many scientific discoveries and their attendant shifts in thinking have arisen out of a moment of epiphany.

The fundamental nature of an epiphany is that it seems to come unsought and unasked for, without a person having to work for it.

Some people call it a moment of grace. I say "seems to," because it often comes during a period when, in fact, a person is working on a problem, and then they have a sudden insight into the problem. That sudden insight is an epiphany.

One of the hallmarks of an epiphany is that it brings about a permanent change. Once you know something, you can't unknow it, and new knowledge brings greater understanding and a way of thinking that can lead to new discoveries. This is why I call this method the epiphany method: because it involves doing some preparatory work, setting the process in motion, and then waiting for forgiveness to come in the form of an epiphany. I have used this method many times and it works wonderfully well.

The epiphany method can work for any person or situation you want to forgive. Some time will elapse between when you start the process and when you receive that epiphany, but all you need to do is start the process. After you start the process, you may think nothing is happening, but one day, you will find yourself thinking about that person, and you will suddenly realize something that gives you a new understanding of them. That new understanding brings a sense of peace to your heart. Or you will find you suddenly have no hard feelings toward them; you've let go of those feelings and thoughts and that person; you've allowed them to be themselves.

Sounds great, right? The one catch to this method is that you cannot know when you will have that moment of epiphany. It could happen soon after you set the process in motion--very soon, in some cases. Or it could take months or even years to reach that moment. But the overall process, though slower, can just as surely bring you to a state of forgiveness, so it is a good method to use for those particularly tough cases when you are finding it hard to forgive, or when you don't want to use the three-step method, or when an entire situation seems too complex to tackle.

In my experience, these moments of epiphany bring about a permanent change for the better. Until you experience your first forgiveness epiphany, it can be hard to understand how profound those moments are. When I've had these moments, I've felt a relaxation spread through my entire being, and I've felt all my previous thoughts and feelings of anger, judgment, and resentment fall away forever. Gratitude for the release of those old feelings fills my heart. It's a wonderful feeling, one not to be missed, and it seems miraculous both because of how deep and permanent the change is, and because I feel like I put so little effort into it. I think these moments of epiphany are can also be called moments of grace.

How To Set an Epiphany in Motion

To set the epiphany method in motion, you will still need your list of people and situations to forgive (the list you created in Chapter 7), and you will still need to be willing to forgive, as described in Chapter 8 under the first step of the three-step method. But after that, you will be doing things differently. One difference is that, although I recommend using the three-step method for one person at a time, you can set as many epiphanies in motion at a time as you like.

Here are the epiphany method's three easy steps:
1. Set a goal.
2. Ask for a resolution.
3. Wait for an epiphany.

Set a Goal

To set a goal, choose someone or something from your list (the list you created in Chapter 7) that you want to forgive and are willing to forgive. As with any forgiveness method, your willingness to forgive is an essential part of this method.

If you haven't already created a list, read Chapter 7 on creating a list of people to forgive. Then choose someone from that list. Although for other forgiveness methods I recommend starting with someone who might be easier to forgive, for this method, someone in the high-intensity portion of your list could be a good choice.

As an optional secondary goal, set a time, date, or even year by which you wish to have arrived at forgiveness toward that person. Bear in mind that you might reach the epiphany earlier or later.

Ask for a Resolution

The next step is to mentally ask for the epiphany; that is, ask for a resolution to come to you for your feelings toward that person or situation. According to your beliefs, you can choose to think that this resolution will come from your subconscious mind working on the problem, or from outside help of some form, or from your soul, or some combination of all of these things.

Asking for anything (for that matter, focusing on anything) sets the energies of life into motion to bring that thing to you (or more of it). In asking for a resolution, you are asking for help. As discussed in Chapter 6, asking for help is a way to connect yourself with the web of life that we all dwell within. If you believe in prayer, then ask for assistance in a prayer. Otherwise, say something like this (aloud or silently, as you prefer; though I think there is more strength in saying it aloud): "Whatever help there is in the universe for this task of forgiveness, I ask that it come to me in a way and form that I recognize and can benefit from."

Wait and Observe

After you have chosen someone you are willing to forgive, have opened yourself to the possibility of forgiving them, and have asked for assistance, now you wait and observe.

While you wait, allow your decision and willingness to forgive someone to simmer on the back burner of your brain. As time passes, forgiveness will come to you naturally, in small pieces or large, and not necessarily all at once. Think of it as planting a seed: you prepare the soil, you plant the seed as best you know how, then you leave it alone. You water it now and then, and perhaps remove weeds that might crowd the new plant, but you don't dig up the soil to see if the seed has sprouted. So don't focus on what you've set in motion, and try to set aside any worries about it. But don't try to avoid all thoughts about it either: be open to insights that come to you in regard to that other person.

While you are waiting, you will receive new information and new ways of thinking and feeling about something or someone. The expected result is that, as time passes, one day you may find yourself musing about the issue or person that is bothering you, or possibly about something related to that issue or person. While you are thinking, you suddenly have an epiphany: a new thought or a new understanding about that issue or person, a thought or understanding that brings a new perspective, making some aspect of the situation or person okay to you.

Your epiphany can also come when you are talking with someone about the situation. The person may offer an alternative way of thinking about it: a more optimistic or positive approach that makes sense to you, and that insight will suddenly open the door to forgiveness for the person or situation you want to forgive. Or you might read a passage in a book, or hear a phrase in a movie, or hear a song, that inspires you to think in a new way about the situation.

When this happens, something can widen in your heart and mind, and you will find yourself feeling differently about the person or situation, so that what was troubling you no longer bothers you. You might experience a sense of relaxation in your mind and heart toward that person or situation. You might even find yourself feeling better about an entire group of people, or type of person.

Because of the nature of an epiphany, you might be inclined to dismiss the triggering thought or inspiration; you might tell yourself it was not important. But please don't. If you do so, you'll be throwing away a gift that has come to you in answer to your desire to forgive. Instead, accept the new way of thinking, that new perspective on the person or situation.

As you live your daily life, that change in perspective will affect other, unexpected areas of your life. It can help you deal with similar people or situations in an entirely different way.

Chapter 11

Forgiving Yourself

We often focus on others and what we need to forgive them for. We each also have a lot that we've done that we are not proud of, or that we hold against ourselves. If we forgive ourselves, we could feel better, though sometimes we don't think of forgiving ourselves.

"Stop this. For your own sake."
Commander Shepherd, Mass Effect 2

Just as harmful (or perhaps more so) as not forgiving others, is not forgiving ourselves. We make mistakes, as all human beings do, and sometimes those mistakes have serious consequences, consequences that perhaps we didn't intend, but that affected others or ourselves nonetheless. When that happened, we judge and blame ourselves. We blame ourselves for not understanding something, or for not forgiving, or for causing a situation, or for being in that situation. We might also criticize ourselves for having bodies that don't fit our ideals, or for not doing things we think we should be doing in the ways we think we should do them. And then we criticize ourselves for criticizing ourselves. And the fault-finding goes on. Meanwhile, we hold all this against ourselves. We cringe internally whenever our thoughts turn toward whatever we did that we are not proud of, or aspects of ourselves that we don't like.

All that has to stop. Just as not forgiving others affects our physical, emotional, and mental health, even more so does not forgiving ourselves. We have to be our own advocates. We each must be on our own side. If we are not on our own side, we present ourselves as sacrificial lambs to others; we are unhappy with ourselves, and we make life worse for ourselves (and others) than it has to be.

This isn't to say that we are completely innocent or harmless. We all have a lot to answer for. Do we have to live with what we've done? Yes, of course. But should we or can we forgive ourselves? The answer is a resounding "Yes."

Many people find it easier to forgive others than to forgive themselves. It can be easier to find something positive in someone else's transgressions against us than it is to do the same for ourselves. But it is not only possible to forgive ourselves, it is necessary.

To forgive ourselves, we need to apply the three-step process of forgiveness to ourselves, with one addition: we also need to make amends in whatever ways we can.

It won't be easy to forgive yourself for some things. That's because you know yourself best, and you know when you truly messed up. And if you have been holding something against yourself for a long time, that habit of self-condemnation will be hard to break. But for your own sake and the sake of others around you, I encourage you to try. When you work on forgiving yourself and changing how you think using the techniques in this book, your health, mood, and attitude can improve greatly, and how you treat others can change for the better, which in turn can improve your relationships.

Blaming Ourselves Needlessly

Sometimes, to forgive ourselves, we need to get out of the habit of blaming ourselves. By that, I mean we need to stop telling ourselves (or others) that something was our fault and that we deserve some kind of punishment, whether that punishment be a withholding of something from us (such as affection or love or a promotion at work), or a taking away from us (such as something physical, or our children if we have them).

But we aren't always at fault or, when we are, the punishment we think we deserve is far more drastic than the situation calls for. In fact, I don't think anyone deserves punishment; just correction in the sense of making a change in what they are doing and how they are doing it, and also making amends as appropriate.

If you find that you habitually blame yourself and feel you are at fault, start being aware of all the ways in which you do that. The next time you find yourself blaming yourself, take a few minutes to look at the situation as objectively and rationally as you can. Ask yourself,

- Are you really the one to blame?
- If you feel you have some responsibility in the situation, how much of it is truly yours?
- Is there anyone else involved who might also have had some part in bringing about the situation?
- Was there another choice you could have made that would have resulted in a better outcome?
- Are you blaming yourself because you think someone else would blame you? (I.e., are you looking at yourself through someone else's eyes?)
- Is there another way you can look at the situation that makes it a bit less awful to you? Have you ever heard the expression "awful-izing"? It means to find the worst possible thing that can happen, or the worst possible interpretation of a situation, or a person's actions. It arises out of a habitual turn of mind toward the negative. But that can be changed. Review the section on finding a gift in every situation (in Chapter 4), and ask yourself if you can apply those principles of thinking to this situation.
- Is there a gift in the situation? For example, did you learn something that you might not have learned any other way, or did a relationship change for the better because of the situation?
- Is this something you normally blame yourself for? (I.e., do you regularly blame yourself for this sort of thing?)
- Can you think of a time in your past, perhaps in your childhood, when something like this happened and you blamed yourself for it? Or someone else did? If so, back then, were you really to

blame, or were you taking on someone else's opinion of whether you were to blame?

If it is helpful, keep a "Blame Journal"—a journal in which you record each time you blame yourself, what you are blaming yourself for, and your answers to the questions above. Use these questions to determine whether you have truly transgressed. Each time you do this, you may start to see a pattern. You will certainly start to gain insights into the way you think about yourself, and start to see ways in which you can look at yourself more positively.

Each time you blame yourself, and find, through asking yourself these questions, that you truly didn't do anything wrong, or perhaps what you did wasn't as bad as you initially thought, let go of your self-blame. If you find that you did do something that you need to make amends for, or forgive yourself for, then use the techniques of forgiveness to start to see yourself in a better light as described in the next section.

Forgiving Ourselves for True Transgressions

When you have truly done something you feel bad about, you need to forgive yourself. In that case, you can apply the three-step process to yourself. Although you can also use the epiphany method for forgiving yourself, I recommend only using that in conjunction with applying the three-step method of forgiveness to yourself.

Because you are applying the three-step method specifically to yourself, here is a recap of the three steps with your self-forgiveness in mind. (If you need to, review Chapter 8 before proceeding.) When forgiving yourself, I recommend that you focus on just one incident to forgive at a time. You can also use this method if you are seeking to forgive yourself for something that you are (for example, something about your appearance that you don't like, or a personality trait you are unhappy with).

1. You've already chosen yourself as the person to forgive. Be willing to forgive yourself (for one incident or situation at a time.)

2. As described in Chapter 8 (under "Step 2: Create a Narrative" on page 129), write a narrative of the incident you are forgiving yourself for.

3. Now look at what you did with fresh eyes, as described under "Step 3: Look at the Situation With Fresh Eyes" on page 133. Especially, without making excuses for yourself or minimizing the harm you might have done, look for positive ways to view what you did. Is there a gift in the situation for you? Did you learn something from it? If you have just now gained new insights while going through this process for yourself, that counts as a gift.

As part of this step, if you harmed someone else, did you apologize (at the time or afterward), and did you make amends as far as was possible? If you didn't, consider asking for forgiveness from the person or people you harmed. For details on that step, see Chapter 13 on asking for forgiveness.

Chapter 12

Forgiving Our Parents and Family Members

Because our parents and other family members have been with us the longest (even if they've been absent, that absence has been with us a long time), we can find it hardest to forgive them. We can have a lot to forgive. But first we need to become aware of what constitutes an occasional lapse on our parent's part, and what constitutes true harm. With greater awareness, we can more easily forgive them. Finally, we also need to heal the harm that was done.

"Children begin by loving their parents;
as they grow older they judge them;
sometimes they forgive them."
Oscar Wilde, The Picture of Dorian Gray

In Chapter 3, I mentioned that forgiving our parents and family members is different in many respects from forgiving others. Whatever our family members did was not likely to have been a one-time or occasional thing; instead, it would have been something they did consistently, even pervasively, throughout our childhoods. When it comes to people who aren't family, you can always end a friendship, or stop speaking with your neighbor, or move, or change jobs, but you can't escape family so easily.

What happened in our childhood will have affected our entire life as a child, and since then, it will have been informing and coloring our ideas about ourselves, everything we do, every interaction we have with others, our personal relationships (especially any committed relationships), and our relationships with our children (if we have any).

For these reasons, forgiving family members can be deeply difficult, and requires thoughtfulness and love. Although this kind of forgiveness could take an entire book of its own to cover thoroughly, in this chapter I cover at a high level everything you might need to know.

This chapter describes the difference between normal parental lapses (that might have hurt, but that weren't abuse) and childhood abuse. It then lightly touches on how childhood abuse affects us when we grow up, and how forgiveness can help, but won't always take us all the way to healing the harm we took. If your childhood was filled with more than the normal amount of pain, in particular pain from some form of abuse, then you can start taking steps to relieve yourself of the burden of pain, humiliation, anger, resentment, fear, and self-hatred that arises out of such a childhood.

This chapter concludes with some practical things you can do to raise your awareness of what happened and how it affected you, and how to get started on forgiving your parents and other family members.

Normal Childhood Hurts

In many cases, it isn't so much what our parents and other family members said and did, as it is how we thought about and reacted to what they did. In those cases, we may have taken on a hurt from something that was what I will call "normal" childhood hurts. We can recover from these normal hurts and forgive those who inflicted them more easily than we can from true abuse. These normal hurts come from things that happened to us only sometimes and weren't part of a pervasive, long-term pattern of abuse. For example, some of these normal childhood hurts can come from

- being yelled at occasionally
- every so often being denied something we wanted
- having our opinions or needs ignored or dismissed once in a while
- sometimes being left out of a sibling's plans

Note that the important part of these events is that they only happened occasionally. These things aren't optimal, but they do happen to every child, even in the most loving families.

What is a healthy, healing way to think about the hurts we took from such occurrences? Our parents may have been, on the whole, loving and well-meaning, but they might not have known how best to love us. This is especially true if there was a personality mismatch, so that our parents didn't understand us and therefore didn't know how to determine what our needs were, let alone fill those needs.

Also, like everyone else on this planet, parents are flawed human beings, and make mistakes, and aren't always on their best behavior. Yet if they are usually loving and respectful to their children, and meet their children's needs most of the time, then they are good parents.

Other normal childhood hurts from our parents can include not having been allowed to go somewhere our parents felt was unsafe, or having to live with strict rules about where and when we could go places and who we could have as friends. Usually our parents had such rules because they loved us and wanted us to be safe. Even if our parents were strict, if they were consistent about it and didn't play favorites with our siblings, we can learn to see the love they held for us.

Other family members may also have said or done things that hurt us. But if what they did was not cruel or abusive, and if their overall interactions with us were loving, then although we may have felt hurt when it happened, we can also learn to see the love that they held for us.

We can also learn to see that our siblings were children too and could only be expected to behave as children. They couldn't be what they were not: they couldn't act as mature adults because they were immature children.

For such childhood hurts, the three-step method of forgiveness described in Chapter 8 (or the epiphany method described in Chapter 10, or both methods) may be all you need to use to forgive your parents or other family members. Or you can add the suggested additional steps to take that are described under "Forgiving Your Parents and Family" on page 204.

Recognizing Childhood Abuse

Surprisingly often, people are not aware that they have been abused; they think that what happened to them was normal or acceptable. They may have been aware on some level that what was going on wasn't right, but, because they were children and needed to rely on their parents for survival, they may have deeply buried their hurt, anger, confusion.

Like many people, you may believe that your childhood was "fine"; you may believe there was no abuse and you yourself were the problem, and, unlikely though it is, that *could* be the case. But the more likely scenario is that you were abused and that your childhood was far from fine. What happened to you wasn't right.

As the old saying goes, "Where there's smoke, there's fire." If you have a gut feeling about your childhood or about things that may have happened to you when you were a child, there almost certainly is something there. Also, when abuse is inflicted on one child in a family but not on another, the sibling is also being abused, but in a different way.

Abuse can come in many different forms, including

- physical, such as hitting or beating
- verbal, such as saying cruel things (belittling, berating, humiliating, screaming)
- emotional, such as invalidating a child's thoughts, opinions, experiences, or existence, or subjecting a child to unrealistic expectations, such as expecting children to perform a new task perfectly the first time they are asked to do it
- neglect, physical or emotional, such as withholding food, not providing a sanitary environment, or not meeting the emotional needs of a child
- abandonment, such as a parent leaving or dying
- sexual, such as having sexual relations with or making sexual comments to a child

Once you educate yourself about what abuse is, you might start to see your childhood (and yourself) in a new light. Although it is perhaps obvious what physical abuse is and how it is harmful, some forms of abuse are often not recognized as abuse. Especially if you experienced verbal or emotional abuse, you may be telling yourself that what you experienced wasn't abuse. You might be saying "Isn't it normal for parents to say things like that?" No. And verbal and emotional abuse are just as harmful as other forms of abuse.

With verbal and emotional abuse,because that kind of abuse is "just" words and leaves no outward injuries, a child (and the adult that child becomes) may feel that what happened isn't important or even that it wasn't abuse at all. Such children can start believing that they deserve to be treated that way. And because that kind of abuse usually happens in private, the child is trapped and feels hostage to the parent or family member who is inflicting the abuse. Often the abusing parent or parents present a "perfect family/perfect parent" facade to those outside the family, so the children in that family feel they have no one to turn to for help because they fear no one will believe them.

Other Forms of Abuse

Other forms of abuse include neglect, abandonment, and sexual abuse. Neglect can take different forms. When parents have the financial means to feed, clothe, and house their children properly, but don't do so, that's one form of neglect. Another form of neglect is to act as though their children aren't there. Parents who neglect their children this way ignore their children's needs for validation and praise. They'll ignore their children's accomplishments, look the other way or change the subject when their child tries to share something that is interesting or exciting to their child, keep their distance physically by not hugging or holding their child, and spend all their time engaged in other activities rather than spending any time focused on their child. The book, *The Nanny Diaries*, by Emma McLaughlin and Nicola Kraus, which is fiction but is based on fact, depicts this kind of neglect in some detail.

If a parent wasn't present in our lives, that also affects us. Whether they abandoned us by leaving our lives forever or by choosing not to be an active part of our lives after a divorce, that abandonment hurts, leaving us wondering what we did to make them go away and why our parents don't love us anymore. As children, it seldom occurs to us that we weren't at fault. Instead, our trust and sense of self are affected; we have a hard time creating relationships with others, and don't think we can be worth much.

If one or both parents died, we can see that as abandonment as well. However much we tell ourselves as adults that of course our parents couldn't prevent themselves from dying (unless they killed themselves), when we are children, we see that death as abandonment. We might also feel guilty for being angry at them for dying, or feel guilty for still being alive when they are dead.

Sexual abuse takes many forms, from exposing a child to inappropriate words, books, and images, to having sexual relations with a child. Sexual abuse is a very deep betrayal. All children have the right to be safe, especially in their own home; sexual abuse makes not just their home, but their bodies, unsafe. As with other kinds of abuse, but even more so, children who are being sexually abused feel ashamed, as though they are at fault. And like other forms of abuse, sexual abuse leaves deep scars.

Abuse from Other Family Members

In addition to parents, we might also have had other family members who abused us in some way: they frightened us, were harsh and unloving, or sexually abused us, but because they were a sibling, aunt, uncle, or cousin, we thought we were "supposed" to love them or let them treat us that way. (Especially if our parents were aware of what was going on, but chose to ignore it; or, worse yet, aided the abusive family member. That gave us the message that we were somehow in the wrong and that there was no help to be found.)

If our parents ignored the fact that we were being abused by someone, perhaps by a close family member, that made the situation even harder. By ignoring the abuse and allowing it to continue, our parents were condoning it, sending us a terrible message of what they thought we deserved.

Uncaring, Incapable, and Unloving Parents

Another source of pain in our childhoods is having parents who fall into other areas of neglect or abuse.

- Our parents may have loved us; just not very much, or at least not enough to do the right thing by us.
- Our parents might have loved us but were incapable of being good parents.
- Hard though it is to fathom how it is possible, some parents simply don't love their children. Worse yet, some of these unloving parents want to, and do, harm one or more of their children.

For any of these types of parents, we can learn to understand what they were going through, forgive them, and start working on the harm they did to us.

Parents Who Don't Care Enough

Let's take a look at parents who don't care enough to do their best for us. These parents make sure their children are fed and clothed, and even spend time with their children, but they habitually do one or more things that they know they shouldn't, things that hurt their children. If you experienced parents like this, It could be that you know you were hurt, but at some point you've been told that your parents did the best they could. This statement is very damaging. It places blame on you for being hurt by what your parents did or didn't do, and absolves them of any responsibility for what they did.

Your parents may indeed have tried to do their best, but if they harmed you, then your pain is real and those who harmed you need to be held accountable for that. It is a parent's duty to educate him or herself on how to be a good parent and on what a child's needs are. It is a parent's duty to keep his or her child safe from harm as far as possible. If your parents did something harmful that could have been avoided by educating themselves, then they weren't doing their best.

Sometimes parents know better but hurt their children anyway because they either don't care enough to do the right thing, or they can't help themselves because of pain from their own childhoods, or they enjoy hurting people.

Here's an example of parents who knew better but did active harm to their children because they didn't care enough to do the right thing for their children. In the 1990s, my then-husband and I had dinner at the house of a young couple he knew. This couple had two very young children—a boy and a girl around the ages of 4 and 6.

When it was time to put the children to bed, the mother was only gone for a few minutes. When she returned, I remarked in astonishment at how easily she had been able to put both children to bed so quickly. I told her our own daughter required a lengthy bedtime routine to get settled, a routine that involved reading aloud to her and singing to her and talking with her about her day. This bedtime routine took about an hour.

The mother responded that she used to do those things, but, she said, "it took too long." So every night she gave her children a sedating over-the-counter cold medicine. She said she knew she shouldn't do that, but it was "so easy" and "put them straight to sleep." I was horrified and didn't know what to say. This is an example of a parent who knew better but wouldn't do the right thing. She certainly wasn't doing the best she could.

Your experiences may be different, but you almost certainly know that something wasn't right with some aspect of what your parents did.

Incapable Parents

Some parents, because of their own personal challenges, are incapable of being good parents. They are addicted or mentally ill or otherwise so out of touch with reality that they just can't see, let alone respond appropriately to, what is going on around them.

If our parents were addicted, we saw them spend money on drugs or alcohol, money that should have been spent feeding and clothing us and keeping a roof over our heads. We lived our lives in fear, never knowing whether a particular day would be "normal," or whether we would have to deal with the fallout from our parents' addictions. We might have witnessed a parent lashing out in rage while under the influence, only to have them apologize sweetly to us when they came out of it.

We also lived our lives in shame: we were ashamed of our parents, and, fearing the shame that would follow, we were afraid of anyone finding out. We felt that there was something shameful about us.

If our parents were mentally ill, we might not have realized that something wasn't right with them until later in our childhood. We were confused and frightened by the weirdness and inappropriateness of what our parents did, and by their inconsistency.

These parents may have loved us, but the way we had to live because of their condition will have left scars and a lot of mixed feeling: love, anger, confusion, a lingering fear, and a tendency to follow in our parents' footsteps by getting addicted. Or we may choose people who are like our parents. In *Keeping the Love You Find*, Harville Hendrix provides detailed steps you can take to figure out how your parents affected you and your relationship choices.

Unloving Parents

In addition to parents who don't care enough to do the right thing, some parents don't love their children. I am not talking about parents who truly love their children but just don't know how to be good parents. I mean parents who dislike, even hate, their children, parents who do not have good intentions toward their children, parents who, if they think they can get away with it, will harm their children.

It is a horrible feeling when you realize that a parent doesn't love you; even worse to realize that they deliberately tried to hurt you. In fact, it can be very hard to let yourself see that truth about your parent. But it is necessary, because until you see it, you'll be fighting the wrong battle with yourself and that parent.

My mother was one of those parents. To people outside our immediate family, including close friends and family (aunts, uncles, and cousins), she seemed like a pleasant, well-educated, and agreeable woman who loved her children. But in private she showed a different face to her children. She was abusive, not because she couldn't help herself, but because she enjoyed inflicting pain. Because of this, my childhood, and that of my three older brothers, was filled with terror and pain. I was a particular target for my mother, and lived in fear of my life and my well-being from infancy. She did her best to obliterate my sense of self and self-worth.

No one outside our family had a clue, and because we moved every six months or so, no one had a chance to figure it out, so we were on our own.

It was a gut-wrenching day when I finally realized that my mother not only didn't love me, she wanted to harm me. I felt as though the floor of the world had dropped away. I realized that everything I thought I knew about my mother was wrong. I went from thinking that I was the problem and that all her actions toward me were justified, to realizing that the opposite was true: I wasn't the problem, she was, and none of her actions were justified

The damage she did ran deep; I am still working on healing the harm done. However, I was able to use the three-step method to forgive her while she was still alive, even though she remained malevolent toward me until the day she died. And if I can do this, you can too.

How Our Childhood Experiences Affected Us

Our experiences as children with parents or family members like those I've been describing were confusing, frightening, and painful. As children, we look up to our parents and other adults as role models. We rely on our parents and relatives to be trustworthy, to keep us safe, and to love, care for, and nurture us. When our parents let us down by consistently failing to be role models, or, worse yet, when they expose us to harm or even harm us themselves, we feel (and are) betrayed and unsafe. As children, we tend to blame ourselves for the pain we feel, and think that how we are being treated is our fault.

This kind of childhood can cause us to doubt ourselves and our true worth. For some of us, our response is to shrink from life and not achieve our full potential. For others, we become like our parents, taking on their prejudices and anger as our own, treating others the same way we were treated, including our family members and our children. Even if we genuinely love our children, we treat them as we were treated, unaware that we are harming them. Or we might swing in the other direction and not give our children enough guidance. Even if we are aware that we were abused and that we took harm from that abuse, we don't know there are alternatives or we don't know how to change our behavior.

If our relationship with a parent or family member was deeply abusive, especially if we received that abuse starting at early age, we will be filled with a maelstrom of painful thoughts and emotions about what happened. We will also have taken into ourselves false beliefs about ourselves, most usually that we are not worthy of love or even life. We might believe that we are wasting valuable food and air that others more rightly deserve, so we never ask for what we want, we always put others first, and we never take care of our own needs. What happened to us also gets in the way of us having healthy, happy relationships with others.

As you educate yourself about abuse, if you recognize that you were abused, then you may want to take steps to deal with it. There are two aspects to dealing with it. Forgiving your parents and yourself is one aspect. The second aspect is healing yourself: learning to value yourself and to know that nobody deserves to be treated the way you were treated, as well as learning to not repeat the abuse by either allowing yourself to be abused or by passing that abuse on to those you love.

Healing the Pain Through Forgiveness

The first aspect involves forgiving both your family and yourself: your family, for having abused you, and yourself because you very likely blamed yourself for the abuse. That forgiveness can take care of the burden of pain, anger, even hatred toward that family member that we carry in our hearts. I know this is possible because I've done it myself, and many others have as well. It can be very healing to arrive at a sense of compassion and understanding for an abusive parent; even to feel a wholesome, unconditional love for that parent, even if we still need to keep our distance to keep ourselves and our own children safe from such a parent.

A useful part of recognizing and dealing with abuse is to learn to understand why the person abused you. A parent, sibling, or other family member can have become abusive because they themselves were subjected to abuse. Or they might not themselves have been abusive, but allowed you to be abused. that doesn't excuse them, of course, but it can help you feel more compassion for them.

Most of the rest of this chapter is about forgiving your parents and other family members. That information is to be used to enhance and expand the methods of forgiveness described in Chapter 8 and Chapter 10.

Healing the Harm Done

The second aspect of relieving our burden of pain is healing our inner self by changing those thoughts and feelings we have toward ourselves that arose out of our experiences. Childhood abuse affects our physical and emotional well-being and how we think about ourselves. It can affect how well we did in school, whether we could make friends, what kinds of friends we had, and so on.

If we internalized an abusive parent's messages, so that we think we are ugly, stupid, clumsy, worthless, and unlikeable, then, although forgiving that parent will help relieve our burden, it won't make us stop thinking those things about ourselves. We'll have scars, not always physical, and deep wounds that have not yet healed.

Also, if we were abused as a child, then we may well be repeating that abuse by choosing to be in abusive relationships or by being abusive toward others.

In my experience, forgiving an abusive family member will not heal or change the false beliefs we hold toward ourselves. By the time we become adults, those beliefs are so firmly entrenched that we believe they are the truth about ourselves. Forgiving someone else, or even forgiving ourselves, won't put much of a dent in those beliefs. Nor will forgiving others cause us to change our own behavior or beliefs about ourselves. Our beliefs and our behavior have to be looked at, preferably with the help of a competent counselor. The last part of this chapter provides some resources for healing yourself.

Forgiving Your Parents and Family

To forgive your parents (or a family member), read the following pages from start to finish and do the suggested self-discovery exercises if you want. Then use either or both of the methods of forgiveness described in Chapters 8 and 9 (the three-step method or epiphany method). The three-step process can be more immediate and powerful. If you choose to use the three-step process, when you reach step three, you may wish to revisit the suggestions described in this section to dig a little more deeply into your relationship and experience.

Acknowledge the Harm Done

The first step to forgiving parents and other family members is to acknowledge what they did, acknowledge the harm we took, and be willing to forgive them. As always with forgiveness, this doesn't mean excusing their behavior or saying that what they did was right or saying that our pain isn't real or justified. It means freeing ourselves from the thoughts and feelings we are holding against our parents or family members so that our hearts are lighter and we no longer dwell in that house of pain.

If you have let your parents or other family members off the hook in the mistaken belief that nothing happened, or you believe that you weren't affected by them, or that what they did didn't matter, you may have spent your entire lifetime, or most of it, discovering that, in fact, what they did mattered tremendously and you have been living your life according to decisions you made in your childhood based on how you were treated.

On the other hand, if you have held your parents or other family members in contempt and kept them in a prison in your mind and heart, punishing yourself and them over and over again, then you are well aware that what they did mattered. Maybe you are not letting go of it because you think that if you did, then it would mean they weren't guilty after all.

In either case, you are holding your parents or other family members accountable for your life, and you are allowing decisions you made in your childhood to still run your life now.

Take Steps Toward Forgiveness

To forgive your parents and other family members, try any or all of the following:

- Examine any fears you might have of making mistakes.
- Use an exercise to help you discover what decisions you made when certain things happened to you, and to change those decisions now.
- Use either or both of the forgiveness techniques described in Chapter 8 and Chapter 10 to forgive your parents and other family members.

These are described in more detail on the following pages.

Fear of Making Mistakes

Whatever harm your parents or other family members did, when you were a child, you made decisions about yourself and them as a response to those actions. Those decisions affected you then and have affected you ever since. For example, you may have decided that you were worthless based on your parents' actions—even on one action. That is not the truth about you, but is instead a decision you made about yourself.

At some point, it is time to revisit what happened so you can make different decisions about the events of your childhood. Decisions can be changed. It might take some time and work to get through a lifelong habit of telling yourself that you were worthless, but you can get there. Changing your beliefs about yourself can be difficult, in part because none of us likes being wrong, even when it can mean feeling better about ourselves. Paradoxically, our reasoning at some level goes something like this: "I can't be worth something, because I've decided I'm not, and if I decide now to tell myself differently, then I would have been wrong in my original decision." Or we might fear admitting that we have been wrong about ourselves because we fear the emotions that might arise, such as anger, or regret over having "wasted" our time feeling that way all our lives.

So changing childhood decisions about ourselves and others also involves facing our fear of being wrong or making mistakes. If one of our childhood decisions was that to be wrong meant we were destined for failure and even death (for example, if every time you made a mistake, your parents physically or emotionally attacked you), then the fear of being wrong can be so compelling that we might prefer to keep our original childhood decisions rather than admit that we might have been wrong.

The fear of being wrong can be incredibly powerful. It can drive people to do all sorts of things, good and bad. It can drive perfectionism, and it can drive denial. Facing the fact that you are afraid of being wrong, or admitting to yourself that it is possible that you might have been wrong, can feel like a huge chasm has suddenly opened up all around you, leaving you only the tiniest piece of land to stand on. Everywhere you turn can seem to mean failure, death, even an annihilation so complete that you will be made to be as though you had never existed.

Ultimately, if this fear is an issue for you, then telling yourself that it is not only okay but perfectly normal and not life-threatening at all to make mistakes might not cut it for you. Telling yourself anything from the rational point of view might not resolve this fear. Mind you, it might. If the work you have done otherwise on yourself has approached this issue, however obliquely, then you might be ready to change this decision (that being wrong is life-threatening) more easily.

It can be a huge relief if you are ready to tell yourself this. You can let yourself off the hook in so many ways. When you make mistakes, you can say to yourself, "Yes, I made a mistake and yes, I need to do whatever needs to be done to make amends for it" (if required), and "yes, I am going to learn from that mistake to never make that particular mistake again, but no, it isn't the end of the world." Or your world, in particular.

So how do you work through the fear of making mistakes? You can use the following techniques:

- *Use rational arguments.* Is your fear of making mistakes rational? Is it realistic to believe that it is possible to never make a mistake? Are you telling yourself that you are the only one who makes mistakes, and that therefore you aren't measuring up to a minimum standard that you are sure others are reaching?

- *Give yourself permission to make mistakes.* Sometimes we make mistakes because we are afraid of making mistakes. One sure way to cause someone to make mistakes is to tell them they are making mistakes. They slow down, become hyper vigilant and less productive, and they over-correct. If you give yourself permission to make mistakes, you can relieve yourself of that internal pressure to always do things perfectly.
- *When you make a mistake, ask yourself, "What's the worst possible thing that could happen from this mistake?"* You might find that in the grand scheme of things, the consequences are insignificant.
- *Also when you make a mistake, look at the results of the mistake.* Was it catastrophic, or did something unexpectedly good arise out of it? Could it have been worse? Did you do something right that mitigated any bad effects?
- *Change your thinking about mistakes.* Some people believe there is no such thing as mistakes; that everything is synchronous and that whatever we did that might seem a mistake can, with investigation, be found to have been the perfect thing to happen. I partly ascribe to that theory; I believe we can make mistakes, but that we can make the best of them by, for example, learning not to make that mistake again. If you can look at mistakes that way, it could help.

Look At Your Decisions and Change Them

Use this simple but effective exercise to take a look at the decisions you made about yourself as a result of your interactions with them when you were a child. This exercise can help bring out unexpected correspondences between your childhood experiences and how you think about yourself now. (You can also use this exercise to evaluate past or present relationships. In doing so, you may see how you have chosen a significant other who more strongly resembles one or another significant adult in your childhood.)

What Did I Decide?

The first step is to take a piece of paper and draw four vertical lines, dividing the page into five columns. At the top of the first column on the left, write "Event." At the top of the second column, write "Decision About Myself." At the top of the third column, write "Decision About My Parents." At the tops of the fourth and fifth column, write "Father/Male Influence" (such as father, uncle, older brother, or grandfather) and "Mother/Female Influence" (such as mother, aunt, older sister, or grandmother).

In the first column, write an event from your childhood that was significant to you and for which you still have strong thoughts and feelings. It can be any event--happy, sad, bad, mad. Start with your earliest memories first, and with your most powerful ones. If there was a pervasive pattern of a type of event--for example, if your father yelled at you repeatedly, then record that as a single event, but place a star by it to indicate that it was repeated.

On the same line in the next two columns, write decisions that you made about yourself and your parents as a result of that event. Don't try to analyze or second-guess those decisions; at this stage you are just bringing out the information from deep in your mind so you can take a look at it. In the next section, you will be working with this information.

In the third and fourth columns, place a check mark for each parent that the event is associated with. For example, if your father was involved, but not your mother, put a check mark in the "Father/Male Influence" column. If some other male who was in a role of authority over you was involved, such as an older brother, a stepfather, an uncle, or a grandfather, also put a check mark in that column. If both were involved, put a check mark in both columns.

Keep writing down events and decisions that you made as a result until you feel you have either exhausted your memories or have had enough of this exercise for the moment. Don't feel you have to access all these decisions at first. It can take a while to remember everything. During the entire process of forgiving, you may find yourself remembering more and more of your life as you uncover and release more and more fears, angers, sorrows, and prisoners of your heart.

Why Did I Decide That?

The next exercise to do is to take each decision you made that you wrote down and think about it. Ask yourself why you made each decision. What positive purpose did it serve? Using the event itself as the reason doesn't count. For example, if your father yelled at you repeatedly for making too much noise when playing, and you decided that you were unacceptable to your father, the yelling wasn't the reason for that decision. It was the impetus for you making a decision about yourself, but it wasn't the cause of the specific decision you made. So see what you can figure out about why you made that specific decision. Often, we made a decision that we felt would ensure our survival; whether that decision was to hide who we truly are, or "lay low" and try not to be noticed, or some other decision, we made it to avoid harm.

Also notice the pattern of check marks. Are the check marks distributed evenly? Or did one person get more check marks? Use this information to shed light on yourself. If you are a man and your father/male influence got the most check marks, can you find a correlation between that and your attitude about yourself as a man? (I am not saying there is; just that there might be.) Or toward other men? (And likewise if you are a woman and it was your mother. Or if you are a man and your mother/female influence got the most check marks. Try all permutations.)

If you are a parent, can you find a correlation between that influence from your childhood and yourself as a parent? For example, do you find yourself doing the same things or saying the same things you experienced or heard in your childhood? Or perhaps doing the opposite? If your parents were overly strict and cold, do you try to avoid doing that to your children by being relaxed and warm?

Take a look at other relationships, such as work. Are there similarities between what your parents did and what you experience from, say, managers whom you've worked for in your career? Or how you feel about your parents and your managers? How about other people in your life? Your significant other? Friends? Other family members? Often, for the purpose of healing, we take the patterns of our childhood and re-enact them until we "get" it and revise our decisions we made so our lives are healthier.

What New Decision Can I Make?

Now examine each decision and ask yourself if there was a different one you could have made about yourself or your parents in that situation. Or if there is a different decision that you can make now. There is always a different decision you can make. Let's use the previous example to illustrate this: your father yelled at you for making too much noise and you decided you were unacceptable to your father. You could instead have decided any one of the following:

- I am fine and my father is not. There is something wrong with my father that causes him to yell like this; this has nothing to do with me.

- Just as some fathers like to drink beer or watch football, my father likes yelling; that's just the way he is. This has nothing to do with me.
- My father truly loves me, but he doesn't know how to show it. His yelling has nothing to do with my worth or how he feels about me.

With your situation in mind, write down one or more new decisions that you would like to make now. As you write down these other possibilities, notice how you are feeling. You might feel relief at the thought that one of the possibilities you are coming up with could be a better truth. That's good. That is the start of healing those events.

Next, choose to believe one of those possibilities. You may argue that seeing other possibilities and making different decisions now, as an adult, doesn't help you, but it most definitely can. Our thoughts and actions toward ourselves and others arise out of our beliefs. If we change our beliefs, we change how we think, act, and respond, especially in regard to ourselves. Changing a decision we Mead about ourselves from something based in fear to something based in love and trust can only have a positive, life-enhancing and supporting effect. It heals us from the inside out.

You might be telling yourself that there is no way you could have made those decisions as a child—that those decisions are too adult or mature or wise. Yet I know from personal experience that children make those kinds of decisions about the situations they are in every day. And there is some part of you that is still feeling the feelings of the child you once were, or these events wouldn't be bothering you today. So allow yourself to make a new decision today and know that it is going to affect that part of you that is still hurting from those events and those decisions.

Use One or Both Forgiveness Methods

After you have done all the above, it is very likely that you are more aware now of your childhood issues and of what went on. You might have remembered more about your childhood, or have come to some new conclusions about it. That's great! You've laid an excellent foundation for forgiving your parents or other family members.

At this point you can now apply either the three-step method or the epiphany method (or both) to a chosen family member. For more on those methods, see Chapters 8 and 9.

Healing the Damage

Earlier in this chapter, I provided some exercises that I have found effective in raising awareness of the harm that was done and by whom. You can go a long way toward healing yourself using those and other techniques if you are willing and ready to do so. In addition, I strongly encourage you to seek the help of a competent counselor who practices one of the many effective forms of therapeutic processes. Before you consult a counselor, though, bear in mind that counselors are humans too, with their own prejudices, biases, opinions, and personalities. If you go to see a counselor and you don't have a good rapport with him or her, go see another, and another until you find someone who suits you. (Though if you find you are switching counselors a lot, that might be an indication that you are trying to avoid dealing with something, and you are looking for a counselor who will let you get away with that.)

One therapeutic process that is used successfully to treat physical and sexual abuse, post-traumatic stress syndrome (particularly with veterans), and similar effects is called Eye Movement Desensitization and Reprocessing (EMDR). EMDR has a very high success rate and can be effective in a short amount of time, with lasting results. Once I tried EMDR, I was amazed at how quickly it was able to heal most of the harm my mother had done. To find an EMDR practitioner near you, visit EMDRIA.org.

Another method that many have had good results from, and that you can teach yourself, is called the Emotional Freedom Technique (EFT). EFT is also referred to as tapping. It involves tapping in specific ways on acupuncture meridian points to access and release blocked emotions. Though it isn't as well-researched as EMDR, and some have said that the positive results can be attributed to the placebo effect, it nonetheless has been effective for many. (The placebo effect is when someone is given a medically ineffective remedy and is told that it is an effective way to treat whatever ails them. In a large number of cases, that person gets better. The end result is the same: they are healed, by what agency is left to the imagination. I believe we heal ourselves using the power we contain within us that reaches toward life.)

If neither of these methods appeal to you, keep looking until you find someone or some method that does appeal. Have faith in your ability to heal, and give yourself time to heal.

Chapter 13

Asking For Forgiveness

Because we are human, we have trespassed on another person's good will; we have taken advantage of someone; we have done something careless or thoughtless. Some of us have done worse: we've physically harmed someone, stolen from someone (even if it was "just" office supplies from our employers), lied in a way that caused harm (though some argue that all lies cause harm), or otherwise done something harmful. For forgiveness to be complete, in addition to forgiving ourselves, we need forgiveness from those we have harmed.

"The greatest achievement in my life in terms of morality is that I can apologize to someone I have wronged. I can bow my head and ask for forgiveness. I think everyone should learn to do this. Everyone should realize that, far from humiliating, it elevates the soul."

Mstislav Rostropovich, Russian cellist

The other side of the coin of forgiveness is that, rightly or wrongly from your perspective, other people will also have taken injury from things you have said or done. Or, you might know you have hurt someone, possibly deeply. What do you do when someone in your life needs to forgive you, or when you want to apologize to someone?

First, you can start with an apology. For some people, it is especially difficult to say the words, "I'm sorry," or "I apologize." It takes a lot of strength and courage to set aside our pride and fear and say those words. It doesn't help that when we apologize, we are often met with a response that rubs our noses in what we did wrong. "You're sorry? Yeah, you *better* be sorry!" Anticipating this kind of response makes it hard to apologize. However, whatever the anticipated response, it is important that we go ahead and do it.

Before you apologize, ask yourself whether you genuinely want to apologize, or whether you feel someone is forcing you to apologize. Sometimes when someone thinks you should apologize, you are fairly certain that what you did wasn't wrong. You can find more about that later in this chapter.

If you are sure you want to apologize, take some time to think through what it is you want to apologize for. When you apologize, never add a phrase starting with the word "but" to your apology; that "but" negates everything that came before. (For example, saying something like, "I'm sorry for what I did, but you asked for it," is not an apology; it's an attack.) It's hard to make a perfect apology, but a sincere, heartfelt attempt can be very effective. Yet even if you do apologize perfectly, be prepared to catch a lot of flack.

Apologizing in Five Steps

The five steps to apologizing are as follows.

1. Contact the person to arrange a meeting.
2. Prepare yourself for the meeting.
3. Come to the meeting on time or a bit early.
4. Apologize and ask for forgiveness, then listen.
5. Whatever you promise to do to make amends, do it.

Contact the Person

Contact the person, say you owe them an apology and amends, and ask if they would be willing to meet with you so you can apologize. If that person's answer is "yes," schedule a meeting at a place and time that you know won't be stressful for either of you. Choose a place that affords you some privacy, so that both of you can freely express yourselves.

A serious note of caution: Make sure you are safe. If you fear that the other person might harm you or themselves, do whatever it takes to make sure you are safe--bring someone else along, make sure the place is safe (perhaps somewhere public), and tell someone else where and when you are going and arrange a regular check-in time (for example, say you will call your friend every hour). Or don't go at all. Trust your instincts, and if you have a bad feeling or are getting some red flags, don't go. Though it is less effective, in such cases it is better to apologize at a distance than to open yourself to injury.

Also, be aware that if the other person has also done injury to you in any way, whether physical or otherwise, your apology may well bring out a level of anger and violence that is out of proportion to the situation. This is because it is human nature to demonize someone we've done an injury to. This isn't the book to go into this aspect of human nature; just be cautious and aware that things can blow up. If you fear harm, consider making your apology over the phone. Again, communicating by phone is not as effective as communicating in person, but it can be safer.

Prepare Yourself for the Meeting

Take some time to mentally go through the situation, doing your best to be objective and to see both sides of the situation. Ask yourself what you could have done differently, or what you could have done that you didn't do. Don't do this from the perspective of beating yourself up over what you did; do it instead as a learning precess, to make sure you understand what you did and why you did it so you don't repeat the same mistake. Use these new awarenesses in your apology.

Also ask yourself if there is anything you can do now that could make amends for what you did. If it is helpful, take notes or write out what you want to say so that you can make sure to say it all. Writing out what you want to say while you are alone and calm can help you stay on track if the meeting gets stormy. If you think there's a good chance the other person may storm out, write your apology as a letter and bring that letter with you. Hand it over to them at the start of the meeting and ask them to read it later, when they are calm. In your letter, express your belief in the possibility of healing the rift.

Come to the Meeting on Time

Come to the meeting on time or arrive a little early. Never be late to this kind of meeting!

Apologize and Listen

At the very start of the meeting, make your apology and ask for forgiveness. Don't let it wait. Start by briefly explaining what you think the situation is, what you think your part in it was or is, and why you think you owe an apology. Then apologize. Be sincere, and don't justify your actions or blame the other person in any way. Present your plan to make amends. As with the letter, express your belief in the possibility of healing the rift. After you apologize, ask if there is anything else (aside from your sincere and heartfelt apology and your offer to make amends) that that person would like you to do. Also ask if there is anything that person would like to say about the situation.

Then listen. Be prepared to stay calm in the face of a lot of emotions. You may face blame and recriminations. That's okay. You are there to give the other person the opportunity to have his or her say, and to forgive you--a rare and wonderful gift for both of you. Part of that gift is you not getting defensive or angry, but instead just listening. If you can manage this, you'll feel good about yourself. The other part of the gift is that you are giving them the space in which they can express themselves to you without it turning into a fight. They might need time to move through their emotions, and by "time," I mean hours, days, weeks, possibly even months or years. That's their journey.

If, after listening, you need to add something to your apology, do so.

Whatever You Promise to Do, Do It

Whatever you promise to do, whether to make amends, or to make changes in your behavior, do it immediately (or as soon as possible). Promising to do something and then not doing it just makes matters worse.

Making Amends

Another part of apologizing is making amends. Making amends means doing the best you can to make it right. If you broke something, fix it or replace it. If you said something cruel or mean about someone and they found out about it, go to the people you said those things to and apologize as well. If you let someone down by repeatedly promising to do something and then never doing it, do what you can to keep your promises from now on.

You can't always fix things by making amends. If you broke your great-aunt's favorite antique teapot, a teapot that wasn't worth a lot monetarily but that meant a lot to her personally because of the memories it held for her, you can't replace it exactly. But you can do what you can to find a teapot like it. That won't entirely make up for her loss, but it can go a long way. Or if you repeatedly broke someone's trust, you will have to work hard to regain it. You might have to face the fact that you will never earn that trust back entirely.

You Are in Control Only of Yourself

None of us is in control of another's thoughts and feelings. Because of this, there isn't anything you can do to force someone to forgive you. Nor would I recommend doing so even if it were possible to force someone; overriding another's free will, or attempting to, is one of the worst crimes a person can commit.

However, although you can't control others, you are in control of what you say and do. If you know someone has taken injury from something you have said or done, you can ask forgiveness, if you feel that is the right thing to do.

This is where it gets tricky, though. What if the person doesn't want to forgive you? I think we all understand how that can be, and at this point in this book, I think you have a good idea of how hard it can be to let go of the pain, hurt, and anger over something someone said or did. In the same way, just as it can be hard for you to forgive, it can be hard for the other person to decide to forgive you. And then it takes time for them to move through the pain and emotions associated with the situation. If the situation wasn't too severe, it might not be so hard or take much time to do this. On the other hand, it could take quite some time—days, weeks, months, even years—for that person to come to a place where they are willing to forgive you, and then more time to fully move through the hurt and come to trust you again. And they may never get there.

Four Situations for Asking for Forgiveness

Here are four possible situations for forgiveness:

- You want to apologize and ask for forgiveness, and the person is willing to hear that apology.
- You want to apologize and ask for forgiveness, and the person is unwilling to hear that apology. Furthermore, they may not want to have anything to do with you ever again. Or, they may no longer be around to apologize to (they may be out of touch or they may have died).
- You admit to yourself you should apologize, but you don't want to because of pride or stubbornness or fear of consequences.
- You don't think an apology is needed.

You Want to Ask Forgiveness

Let's start with the easiest situation: you have accepted responsibility for what you did, you want to ask forgiveness, and the other person is willing to hear you out.

Important! Never ask someone else to convey your apology. That person, no matter how well-meaning, cannot convey the apology as well as you could, and may garble it or make the situation worse (unintentionally or intentionally). A few times, I have trusted someone to convey messages between myself and a friend who was angry at me, and it has never come out well. In some cases, the go-betweens meant well, but introduced their own opinions of what was going on, which was seldom helpful. In other cases, the go-betweens deliberately stirred the pot.

For example, I once depended on someone I trusted to try to heal a rift between myself and a friend over something she had done. I only discovered much later that the "trusted" person was intentionally telling inflammatory lies to each of us about what the other person had said. He knew he could get away with it because we weren't talking with each other, so we weren't able to compare notes with each other about what we said and what he said we had said. By the time I figured it out many months later, the friendship was irreparably dead.

Of course, my friend was also responsible for what she had done to cause the rift and for healing it as well. And we could both have been more willing to speak with each other directly and less willing to believe the bad things being attributed to each other. But since she didn't accept that responsibility, and since I trusted our go-between, healing the rift just wasn't going to happen.

The lesson learned is to always, always, talk directly with the person you are having difficulty with; never use a third party. And as much as possible, talk with that person face-to-face, so they can hear your tone of voice, read your body language, and see your facial expressions, all of which can make the conversation better. When you do this, try to hold in your heart and mind a feeling of love (or at least like) toward that person. Before your meeting, remind yourself of all the things you like about them, and remind yourself why you are apologizing to them. You are seeking to help them and you to heal; you are seeking resolution and closure; you may be seeking to restore a cherished relationship.

What if the Person Doesn't Want To Forgive?

If the person doesn't want to speak with you, let alone accept an apology, be patient. It could be that your relationship is irreparably damaged, and that is just something you will have to live with. If there is any way to convey your apology anyway—perhaps by a handwritten letter—then do so.

Sometimes there's nothing you can do about what someone else is thinking about you or has done to you. It has been rare, but a few times in my life, I've had friends drop me as a friend. Most of the time, I know what happened or why they did it—maybe not exactly why, but close enough. In one case, it was completely my fault. I did something that I shouldn't have done, and it hurt a friend deeply. In other cases, the reasons were a mystery to me. If I had done something, I didn't know what, and those friends never talked with me about it. So I had to live with the fact that I had lost that friendship without knowing why.

In some cases, a friendship has run its natural course and is over. People can fall away as friends because of life circumstances—moving, changing jobs, or other such changes, where you and your friend just don't stay in touch. Sometimes it can be a matter as simple as immaturity and not understanding what friendship is, or incompatibility, where neither of you has enough in common to sustain a friendship.

So what do you do? What if you still want to be friends? That's something you'll have to deal with. You'll have to deal with the fact that they don't want to be your friend. And if it was something you did, then you'll have to deal with that too, and work through whatever it was you did. You might need to forgive yourself, using one of the methods described earlier in this book; you might need to forgive them for not forgiving you. In doing so, you can learn something from what happened. If you need to forgive yourself, it could be that what you learn is how not to do it again. You may never be able to restore that relationship and, hard though it may be, that's just something you'll have to live with. At least you won't make that mistake again.

But even if you can't apologize in person, you can still apologize in a way that can help ease your heart. If you are unable to meet with this person, hold an imaginary conversation with them as described in Step 3 of the forgiveness method (in Chapter 8). imagine that you are in a safe, happy place with this person. Give your apology, and listen to what you imagine they would say. If this is the only resolution you are able to achieve, it can still be very helpful.

You Are Afraid To Apologize

What if you admit to yourself you should apologize, but you don't want to? What reasons might you have for not wanting to? Your reasons could include pride, stubbornness, or a fear of the consequences, but fundamentally they are arise out of fear. Because they arise out of fear, these can be tough obstacles to overcome.

Not apologizing because of pride could be because you are afraid of losing face or seeming like you are less in someone else's eyes (or maybe in your own). But it is very likely that others who are involved are fully aware of what you did and the consequences of what you did, and already think less of you for having done it, and even more so because you are refusing to admit it or apologize. It might help to remind yourself of that to counter your fear of apologizing. It takes a great deal of courage to own up to our mistakes, and most people will admire you for it, not think less of you.

The same applies if you don't want to apologize out of stubbornness. Although stubbornness has its place (for example, it can help keep you from being pushed around by other people, and can keep you trying to do something until you succeed), stubbornness for the sake of being stubborn can harm your relationships and cause you to lose out on a lot of good things in life.

If you are afraid of the consequences of apologizing, then ask yourself what you are afraid of. Are you afraid that you will be admitting something that will change your relationship? For example, if you lied to someone and now you need to both tell them about the lie and apologize for it, then that definitely will affect your relationship with them. But ask yourself what kind of relationship you will have if you don't apologize. You have already changed the nature of your relationship by what you did; it is now up to you to do your best to make it better again.

What if No Apology Is Needed?

What if what you have done is perfectly ordinary, and in your eyes doesn't warrant an apology, but the other person has chosen to take offense? Some people just have a hair trigger and there is nothing you can do about it. One time, many years ago, a friend and I were going to carpool to a doctor who lived a few hours' drive away. There was nothing wrong with either of our cars, nor did either of us have any kind of financial difficulty that made it essential that we carpool; we were just going to be efficient by going together (and, of course, we were going to enjoy each other's company, and that of our children).

A few days before our appointment, a work issue came up and I needed to cancel my appointment so I could attend a meeting that day. After canceling with the doctor, I called my friend and told her the situation. I apologized for the short notice, and said she'd have to go on her own. Without a word, she dropped me as a friend. She didn't tell me she was dropping me; she simply did. I only figured it out because she never called me again, she wouldn't answer my phone calls, nor would she talk with me. I never did figure out what that was about; I didn't (and still don't) think that what I had done warranted so severe a reaction. But just as clearly, she thought she had been injured beyond repair of the friendship.

If something like this has happened to you, treat it the same way as the case when someone doesn't want to hear an apology. Even if the other person seems out of line from your perspective, it can help to apologize, or to send an apology. In this situation, once I realized how angry she was, I wanted to apologize for whatever offense it was that I had given without knowing what I had done. It wouldn't have hurt me to do so, and it might have helped soothe whatever was going on inside her. But since she wouldn't even speak with me, and I didn't have any other way to contact her, that avenue was closed to me.

Although similar in many ways, this situation is a little different from the situation in which you have done something and the other person refuses to forgive you. In my example, I had done something that, while not rude or socially unacceptable, still created an inconvenience for someone else. In that case, an apology would have been called for. In your case, you may have done nothing that requires an apology. In that case, it is the other person's issue, and if you can't talk with that person, then you just need to let go of the situation and walk away. If it is within your belief system to do so, release the situation to a higher power.

You can also hold a mental conversation with them, similar to that described on page 155 in Chapter 9. To hold this conversation, imagine that you are somewhere safe with this person. Have a mental conversation with them; give your apology, and listen to what you imagine they would say. Although this may not affect the other person, it can be very helpful for you.

Epilogue

Having read this book, you are now ready to put the principles in it into practice. But first, a few final thoughts for your journey.

"Life is a series of natural and spontaneous changes. Don't resist them; that only creates sorrow. Let reality be reality. Let things flow naturally forward in whatever way they like."
Lao Tzu

Now that you have read this book, take some time to let it all sink in. You're heard many good reasons to forgive, not the least of which is to improve your life, health, and happiness. You've also been given a number of excellent ways of thinking about life and forgiveness that can help you make those improvements.

I understand that, although the principles in this book are simple, they can be challenging to put into practice. Those challenges are worth facing and overcoming, because making these principles a habit can profoundly affect your life. So I encourage you to give yourself the time and grace to learn these principles, and to make their practice a daily habit.

If you find you are bogging down or feeling overwhelmed—and I do understand how very much is in this book, and how very great the changes are that these principles can require—then dial it down. Choose just one of the principles of the forgiving lifestyle described in Chapter 4, and focus on making just that one principle a new habit. Choose just one person to forgive from the list you created in Chapter 7, and don't fret about anyone or anything else until you have forgiven that person. Or, if forgiving that person is proving more of a challenge than you anticipated, set them aside and choose someone else.

Take forgiveness one day at a time. You won't always be able to practice every aspect of the forgiving lifestyle, but each time you do, that is progress toward a life that is filled with acceptance and compassion.

Acknowledgments

No book is ever written in a vacuum. The many people who have flowed through my life, offering me lessons in love and forgiveness, deserve my thanks. In particular, I would like to thank the following with love and gratitude for their positive contributions to my life:

Elisabeth Michaels, my daughter, without whom my life would have been much less than it is.

Jordon Rader, a patient man who has made my life so much better in so many ways.

My brothers, Norman, David, and Peter Michaels, who were islands of sanity and love in the ocean of pain that was my childhood, and my sister, Lynn Karsh, lost for nearly 30 years, who is everything I ever wished for in a sister.

Linda Derose-Droubay, my sister in spirit. I can always count on her to listen to me without judgment, and to offer excellent advice.

Monesh Josan, my brother in spirit. Monesh has often thanked me for my gifts; it is my turn to thank him. With his help (although he didn't know it), I got this book started.

Karen Marshall, a wonderful person who came unexpectedly into my life and has taught me a great deal.

Louise Nicholson and Jolie Mason, two wonderful women who have been my friends for decades. Having intelligent, supportive, and all-around wonderful friends like them gives me a sense of continuity and stability in a life where so much has changed.

Richard Bach, who once told me, in not so many words, that it is better to starve while serving your life's purpose than eat well while not.

Dan Duggan, who once taught religious studies classes at Santa Clara University. From him I first learned what it means to live an examined life. He also taught that there is a gift in every situation; sometimes you have to work to find it, but it is always there. My life is and has been so much richer and deeper for those two lessons.

My first readers, Heidi O'Claire, Jak Schibley, Jolie Mason, Karen Marshall, and Linda DeRose-Droubay, whose insights and excellent suggestions made this a better book.

The members of Silver Ink, my writer's group: Adrienne Small, Carie Hutchins, Dawn Keiser, and Galen Small, for their moral support and sheer awesomeness.

My cats, who are living models of love and living the forgiving lifestyle.

Bibliography
and Resources

Bibliographies and lists of resources are often so long that they lose their value. With too many choices, we often make no choice. In this list, I've only included a few books, Web sites, and other resources. Any of these can lead you to other resources, and of course there is always the Internet.

Coudert, Jo. *Seven Cats and the Art of Living.* Warner Books, 1998.

In this small, excellent book, the author extracts life lessons from her experiences with humans and cats, and shows how so much of what we take away from an experience is influenced by how we think.

Diong, Siew Mann, George D. Bishop, Hwee Chong Enkelmann, Eddie M.W. Tong, Yong Peng Why, Jansen C.H. Ang, and Majeed Khader. "Anger, stress, coping, social support and health: Modeling the relationships." *Psychology and Health*, August 2005, pages 467-495.

This scientific article, just one of many on the topic, is for those who would like to know more about the science behind how our thoughts and emotions affect our health and well-being, and how we can improve our health by more actively responding to anger and stress.

EMDRIA.org. *You can use this site to find out more about Eye Movement Desensitization and Reprocessing (EMDR, which is discussed in Chapter 12).*

On this site you can also discover how EMDR has been successful in treating post-traumatic stress, and you can search for an EMDR practitioner in your area.

Engel, Beverly. *The Emotionally Abused Woman: Overcoming Destructive Patterns and Reclaiming Yourself.* Fawcett Columbine, 1992.
You'll find many books on this subject, but this is one of the best. Although this book is for women, it can also be useful for men. It teaches how devastating emotional abuse can be, how to recognize it, and how to heal from those experiences.

Evans, Patricia. *The Verbally Abusive Relationship: How to Recognize It and How to Respond.* Adams Media, 2010.
This book is an excellent companion to Beverly Engels' book. It describes what verbal abuse is, how to recognize it, and how to respond to it.

Forward, Susan. *Toxic Parents: Overcoming Their Hurtful Legacy and Reclaiming Your Life.* Bantam, 2002.
This excellent book describes what childhood abuse is in all its forms.

Hendrix, Harville. *Keeping the Love You Find: A Personal Guide.* Atria Books, 1993.
In this book, you can find out more about how your childhood perceptions of your parents influence who you choose to be in a relationship with.

Kam, Katherine. "Rein in the Rage: Anger and Heart Disease." (August 15, 2014) http://www.webmd.com/heart-disease/features/rein-in-rage-anger-heart-disease.
This is one of WebMD's numerous medicine-based but very readable articles on health issues.

Katal, Ingrid. *What Is Your Honor Code? The Missing Link to Managing Your Mind.* Simply True Communications, 2007.
Ingrid encourages you to take a look to see if your life is where

you want it to be in every area, and, if it isn't, she provides tools for you to make the changes you want.

Loveisrespect.org.

This excellent site provides information about abuse: how to recognize it and how to deal with it, either for yourself personally or for people you know (such as in the workplace).

Pearson, Michael. "Marine Vet Who Took Grenade Blast for Comrade to Receive Medal of Honor." CNN, May 20, 2014 (accessed May 23, 2014) http://www.cnn.com/2014/05/20/us/medal-of-honor-carpenter/?iref=obinsite.

Schucman, Helen (scribe). *A Course in Miracles*. Foundation for Inner Peace, 1975. All quotes from *A Course in Miracles* are from the 'X' Edition, 2011, ©Foundation for Inner Peace, P.O. Box 598, Mill Valley, 94942-0598, acim.org and info@acim.org.

This book has been one of the most influential in my life and on my way of thinking. Millions of copies of this book have been sold, and it has been translated into twenty-four languages (with more on the way). If you can accept its premise that the material was received intuitively by the author from Jesus, or if you can suspend your disbelief long enough to read this book, you will find powerful, life-changing ideas concerning love, forgiveness, and our true natures.

Tapper, Jake, and Tom Cohen. "Medal of Honor Recipient Conflicted by Joy, Sadness." CNN, February 12, 2013 (accessed May 23, 2014) http://www.cnn.com/2013/02/11/politics/medal-of-honor/.

wikihow.com. "How to Use the Emotional Freedom Technique (EFT)" (August 15, 3014) http://www.wikihow.com/Use-the-Emotional-Freedom-Technique-(EFT).

Wikihow is an excellent resource for many life topics.

Made in the USA
San Bernardino, CA
15 November 2014